Making Your Own Preserves

Jane and Rob Avery

Making Your Own Preserves

Prism Press

Published in the U.K. in 1980 by
PRISM PRESS
Sherborne, Dorset,

and in the U.S.A. by
PRISM PRESS
P.O. Box 778
San Leandro
California, 94577

Illustrations by Trevor Aldous

© 1981 Jane and Rob Avery

ISBN 0 907061 17 6 (Hardback)
ISBN 0 907061 18 4 (Paperback)

Distributed in the U.S.A. by Interbook Inc.,
861 Lawrence Drive, Newbury Park, California 91320

Distributed in Australia by Doubleday Australia Pty Ltd.,
14 Mars Road, Lane Cove, N.S.W. 2066

Distributed in New Zealand by Roulston Greene,
P.O. Box 33-850, Takapuna, Auckland 9

Distributed in South Africa by Trade Winds Press (Pty) Ltd.,
P.O. Box 20194 Durban North 4016

Typeset by Margaret Spooner Typesetting, Dorchester, Dorset
Printed by Purnell & Sons (Book Production) Ltd., Paulton, Bristol

Contents

What Are Preserves?

In the accepted sense, preserves are fruit and vegetables—or mixtures of fruit and vegetables—that are processed in such a way that they can be stored in jars and bottles for later use. Sometimes—as with pickled onions for example—they will maintain much of their original form. But in other cases the raw material will be chopped, minced, or blended so much as to be barely recognisable.

In practice though 'preserves' is an arbitrary term referring not only to the bottling of fruit and vegetables, but also the drying, salting, and what have you, of a variety of produce.

Apart from freezing—which is highly questionable in a cost effective sense—there are a great many ways in which food can be preserved at home. However, we intend that above all this book shall be practical. So we will concentrate on those methods that the average busy householder with basic kitchen equipment can be expected to try and tackle. The finer points of building your own root cellar, or wind drying your surplus cod fish may make very interesting reading but in practical terms you will be unlikely to actually get round to trying your hand at them. But home food preservation is a fascinating subject, and doubtless from time to time we shall be enticed away from this basic statement of intent. In the main though what you can expect to be reading about are the realistically practical ways to bottle your own jam, marmalade, pickle, chutney, preserved fruit, etc., and to process other edible raw materials for long term storage.

Many of the techniques we shall be describing are traditional ones of long standing; and until comparatively recently a very necessary way of hoarding the plenty of summer against the barren months of winter. For housewives in the remote countryside a well stocked larder was an essential element of survival. In towns too, there was little of the insulation from the natural order of things that we now take for granted. Produce not in season would simply not be available. No road-freighted fruit from the Mediterranean. No strawberries jetted in from Israel. When the hungry gap of winter came, you either went to the store cupboard or went without. So in town and country alike, preserving was a vital part of normal kitchen routine.

But Why Bother With Preserves Nowadays?

Well, basically because we like them. Even with the widespread use of freezers, and the sustained supplies of produce that we are used to finding in the shops nowadays, practically all of us regularly eat preserves of some sort. The main difference today is that some commercial concern makes them for us. And very handsomely we reward them for their efforts. Marmalade, jam, sauce, chutney, pickled onions—all these and others we accept as a normal part of our everyday lives. So we still use preserves whether we realize it consciously or not. It is just that today most of us don't make, or even know how to make, our own.

The Cash Saving

If you make your own preserves you will save a great deal of money. We guarantee you that. Even with small scale home production, and buying your raw materials, you will find they will cost you no more than half the price of those bought in the shops. If you grow your own produce, or gather free ingredients from the wild, the savings will be even greater.

The cost of even quite mundane factory produced preserves is now alarming; particularly when you discover how cheaply they can be made at home. And don't even dare look at the prices of the more exotic offerings. In your shocked disbelief of the asking price, the jar will be sure to slip from your grasp and go crashing to the floor. Then you will have to take out a second mortgage to repay the shopkeeper for the damage you have done. But let's not be too hard on the retailer—or indeed the manufacturer and wholesaler. They have ever increasing labour, distribution, and overhead costs to cope with; and individually their profits are not all that great. On the other hand, nobody forced them to set up in business. So if there is an opportunity for you to side-step the final brunt of all the profit taking—why not do so? You can certainly cut out the manufacturer, wholesaler, and shopkeeper—simply by making your own preserves. Whether you can eliminate the services of the first link in the chain—the grower—will depend on your own particular circumstances. But even if you don't have the space or the inclination to produce most of your own raw materials, there will be wild crops for the gathering, and real bargains in the shops and markets at peak times. Plus of course the chance to economise even further by picking your own at the increasingly popular open fruit farms. Your only expenditure after that—apart from fuel costs and a few minor odds and ends—will be sugar and vinegar. Remember too that as an alternative to freezing, traditional home preserving involves you in no large capital outlay or continual running and maintenance costs.

Manufacturers Additives

Compared with some foodstuffs, commercially produced preserves get off fairly lightly as far as additives are concerned. Many of them have Sodium Citrate added to help stabilize

colour, and nearly all of them contain chemical 'preservatives' to prolong shelf life.

A great deal of concern has been expressed by various writers (present company not excepted) about the way in which manufacturers dose the foods we eat with literally thousands of different chemicals. Here is not the place to go into the matter in any great depth, but take it as fact that very little is known about the effects these additives may be having on us, particularly the inter-reactive effects. It must therefore make sense to avoid as many of them as possible. In practice this is easier said than done. But by eating your own untampered with preserves you will at least be taking a positive step in the right direction.

Factory Food

One of the great delights of good home made food is its fresh wholesomeness. And we use fresh in a dual sense. Not stale, and a new experience. Unlike the bland offerings of the chemifood conveyor belt, each new batch is chateau bottled wine. Always excellent—sometimes excelling. Not the sort of definition that immediately springs to mind when trying to describe factory food. All that usually manages to awaken is the dull response that it probably is edible, and does taste something like the sort of food it is meant to be. Divest it of its pretty packaging and its carefully advertised image, and what are you left with. Cost effective food. Only made saleable by expert presentation and the untruthfully advertised inference that a modern food factory is just a more hygienic version of grandma's farmhouse kitchen. Stripped of any individuality, the ingredients have been reduced to the blandest of common denominators. That is the best that any sort of mass catering ever achieves. As far removed from good old home cooking as any other junk food.

The Satisfaction and Enjoyment

For many people these are the most rewarding aspects of home preserving. Having created something worthwhile, you can now justifiably take your rightful place in the smug ranks of the efficient home economist. With the harvest safely home will come the well earned gloats over a filled to bursting store cupboard. Yours too the almost indefinable satisfaction of having been involved in an old and traditional craft.

In more practical terms though these are just so many fringe benefits. The real pay-off is literally still in store for you. Delicious meal after delicious meal awaits your pleasure.

Another point to bear in mind is that with a store cupboard full of home preserves you will never again be at a loss for a very acceptable little gift for some lucky recipient. Remember too that because they are so superior to factory made preserves the home made variety is a very saleable little commodity; providing useful income either for yourself or for some worthy charitable cause you would like to support.

General Principles

In home preserve making the basic general principle behind all the various methods is to isolate the raw materials from factors that can cause them to go bad. Allowing them to remain in good condition over a period that will far exceed their natural life.

In most cases this isolation is achieved in two distinct steps. Firstly the raw materials are relieved of any possible contamination. Then in this sterile state they are stored in a medium that will inhibit degeneration. One has to say inhibit, because no method of food preservation is indefinite; and nor does it really need to be. All one really wants is to have food put by until it comes back into season—or at least until it is well out of season.

The type of storage medium chosen is dictated by the nature of the raw material and the kind of end product that you want. Doubtless you could store strawberries in vinegar and they might, in a specimen sense, keep fairly well. But common sense would tell you that you would be unlikely to end up with anything that was remotely edible. So the medium itself must be a compatible one, or at least one that will flavour the raw materials in an acceptable way.

The main function of the medium is to protect the raw material from becoming contaminated. This it does quite simply by shielding it from harmful (mostly airborne) influences. Assisting it in this are usually two other elements. The airtight storage container, and a carefully chosen storage environment. What you are doing in all cases though is to keep contamination away from your processed raw material. In some instances retaining very nearly the original taste, in others altering it into an equally acceptable but essentially different end product.

So the mediums in which bottled preserves are stored vary with the character of the raw material and the sort of preserve being made. Sometimes it will be little more than the packaging safely holding the food. For instance, the vinegar in which pickled onions are bottled is not itself consumed. It acts purely as a preservative and flavourer during the bottle life of the pickle. With other preserves—sauce for example—the storage medium becomes itself part of the food and is consumed along with the rest of the brew.

Why Preserved Food Goes Bad

Now that we have roughly established what preserves are, it will be helpful in explaining the various preserving methods if we identify the factors that can spell disaster. Then later on you will be able to see why each stage in their preparation is necessary, and how in turn these necessary stages have influenced the creation of the wide range of preserves that can be made.

There are four main spoilers of preserved food. Yeasts, moulds, enzymes, and bacteria. These exist all around us and are just itching to get involved in home preserving. Happily though, they will all fall foul of our exemplary hygiene standards and our processing and storage techniques.

Yeasts

These are the naturally occuring spores that are present on wild and cultivated fruit. At increased temperatures they sprout into fungal growths that cause fermentation. For wine and beer makers this is a very useful and necessary phenomenon. For the home preserver they are bad news. Luckily they can easily be eliminated due to their inability to survive temperatures above 140 F.

Moulds

These again are fungi-like organisms, but different from yeasts in that during their growth they can produce toxins. Another problem is that instead of relying on sugar for their growth they consume the very acids that are helping with preservation. However, like yeasts they will be destroyed at temperatures above 140 F. The only problem after that will be to stop them regaining a foothold during storage.

Enzymes

Enzymes are present in all animal and plant life; their function being that of a catalyst assisting constructively with normal growth cycles. But kill the animal or pick the plant and they reverse their role rapidly causing decay. However, once that magic 140 F has been achieved their influences are eliminated.

Bacteria

Three different types of bacteria cause the most serious trouble. Those of the Salmonella genus. The Staphylococcus aureus bacteria that cause 'staph' poisoning. And Clostridium botulinum that produces 'botulism' poisoning —the most deadly of the lot.

The heat processing that destroys yeast, moulds, and enzymes will also kill Salmonella bacteria. So that's one problem solved. But the other two need a more persistent application of heat at a higher temperature. Fifteen minutes of vigorous boiling.

Hygiene

Even though we shall be able to eliminate, or at least neutralize elements that can spoil our food, we will still need a very high standard of kitchen hygiene as a back-up safeguard. Common sense will insist that your raw materials will naturally be in perfect condition and clean. But no matter how careful your processing, you will be wasting your time—and risking your health—if insanitary conditions in the kitchen allow recontamination. So everything must be spotlessly clean. You, your kitchen, and the equipment you will be using.

Also remember that even though relatively high levels of heat will destroy harmful organisms, lower temperatures will provide nothing less than an ideal environment for them to thrive in. So be swift and methodical in your work. Don't leave processed or partly processed food hanging around unnecessarily. Get unprocessed food into the kitchen, get it processed, and then get it out again and safely stored.

Acidity

Another important factor in home preserving is the amount of acid naturally present in the food you will be using as a raw material. Technically this is established by what is called a pH (Potential of Hydrogen) rating. But on a less scientific level some knowledge of what it is all about will be helpful because the amount of acid present will have a direct influence on the degree to which it is likely to be (or become) contaminated. The lower the pH rating the higher the acid content, and the higher the acid content the lower the chances of any harmful bacteria (except in the case of enzymes) being able to do their dirty work. For your reference we list below a selection of those foods considered to be 'high-acid' and those considered to be 'low-acid'.

High Acid: Lemons. Gooseberries. Plums. Apples. Grapefruit. Strawberries. Oranges. Rhubarb. Blackberries. Cherries. Raspberries. Peaches. Pears. Pineapple. Tomatoes.

Low Acid: Pumpkin. Carrots. Beans. Spinach. Cabbage. Turnips. Green Peppers. Asparagus. Potatoes. Mushrooms. Peas. Meat. Fish. Shellfish.

What Foods Can Be Made Into Preserves?

In the greengrocery line, practically any that you can grow in your garden or buy from the shops, as well as their cousins growing in the wild. Eggs, herbs, and fungi can also be preserved. So we shall be covering all these and others under the appropriate headings.

How Are Preserves Made?

In a variety of ways, but speaking in very broad terms they can be grouped under four general headings.

The first is what one can call the Jam group. And this covers Jams, Marmalades, conserves, jellies, curds, cheeses and butters. With this type of preserve the fruit is processed in a variety of ways and then cooked with added sugar and water until it reaches the required consistency for storage in sealed jars. Of course other ingredients are included for various reasons, and the specific processing techniques vary considerably. But in very general terms this is what it is all about.

Next is what can be labled the Vinegar group. This takes in chutney, sauce, pickles, and other pickled produce. Here the storage medium is vinegar based, and sometimes the ingredients are cooked and sometimes not. But whole, or in an almost unrecognizable pulped state, the end product is held in vinegar of one sort or the other.

The other main group is bottled fruit and vegetables (a rather confusing term since they are stored in jars not bottles).

The objective here is to preserve fruit and vegetables without altering their natural flavour and shape too much. In the case of fruit the basis of the protective medium is a syrup made from sugar. With vegetables a fairly weak brine solution that will not adversely flavour them too much. The ingredients are cooked or blanched, and added to the syrup or brine in their respective containers. A simplification of the process of course, but that is what basically happens.

Lastly come the odd men out that don't fit into any of the above—perhaps more popular—categories.

In this section we can include Salting, Drying, and Crystallizing—as well as the other odds and ends that are a little more specialized and can't find a home of their own anywhere else.

Salting is one of the oldest methods of preserving food. It is also about the easiest and cheapest to accomplish, requiring little effort, no heat or specialist equipment, and very inexpensive processing materials.

Salted runner beans are probably the most popular example of this type of preserving, and well worth the making too. You can hardly tell them from fresh when cooked. The way in which they are made is typical of most dry salting techniques. The beans are merely sliced as you would for cooking, then layered down with generous quantities of salt in a jar. As simple as that.

Salting and drying overlap a little in some methods of food preservation. The salt acting initially to help draw moisture before taking on its final role of a preservative. But such methods are not really practical for any but specialists; and the kind of drying we shall describe will be the more realistic methods that can be accomplished in the kitchen.

Crystallized and Candied Fruit are something of luxury preserves. The traditional accompaniments to Christmas over-indulgence. They cost a fortune to buy, but the syrup coating technique by which they are both made is merely time consuming and not at all complicated.

Those then are all the general groups of home preserving that can be reasonably expected to be tackled at home. Doubtless, as you go through the book, some types will appeal to you more than others, or suit your requirements more specifically. We tend to make more Jam and Chutney than anything else, but that just happens to be the way we want. But whatever your taste, we are sure that you will find just what you want (or something very like it) among the recipes we have carefully selected for you. One thing is absolutely certain though. Whatever kind of preserves you decide to make, you will never have made enough. There is no such happy state as having made enough preserves.

Equipment and Materials

Equipment and Materials

In the early days of home preserving, before specialist jars were invented, bullock's bladders would be washed in warm water to soften them, then they would be tied on with string to seal the jars. Or mutton fat might be poured in on top of the preserves to form when set an effective air-tight bung. This is of little practical interest to us nowadays—unless you want to organize a preserving through the ages display (which might not be a bad idea)—because happily modern reliable equipment is readily to hand.

But first things first, so let's start with the raw materials.

Selecting Produce for Preserving

In short, all your raw materials should be in perfect condition. Fresh and young and in the prime of life. But that's not to say that slight damage or imperfection is not acceptable if it can be cut away before processing. On the other hand, avoid any over-ripe produce because this will not produce a very good flavour. This is a point to watch with fruit in particular, because if it is over-ripe it will have a diminished Pectin content (we will deal with

pectin a little later on) and you will not get a very good set.

With any particular batch, it will be best if all the raw materials are as uniform as possible. In every way—size, colour, ripeness, whatever. This is desirable for a variety of reasons. Individual parts of a batch will be likely to be all cooked at the same time. Pectin and acid contents will be similar. And they will look better. The last point being particularly important if you are thinking of entering your preserves for competition or for sale.

Sources of Produce

Gardens and Allotments: If you have one, then your own garden must obviously come top of your supply list. You may not be able to grow all you are likely to want to preserve, certainly not fruit like oranges, but there are alternatives to most of the exotics, and the smallest of plots has the potential to provide a high proportion of your needs.

If you don't have a garden of your own, but would still like to do your own growing, most towns and cities have allotment plots that can be rented for very modest annual sums.

Should this prove an impossibility, you could try approaching an elderly neighbour who has found the care of their own garden has become too much for them. They may well be delighted to see it under cultivation again; and the voice of experience will certainly have some helpful advice to give if you are a beginner.

Wild Fruit and Vegetables: Apart from growing your own, gathering from the wild is another possibility. The main problem is one of identification. Everyone knows a blackberry when they see one, but being certain about less obvious varieties can present problems. Which is an important point, because some wild plants or fungi can be poisonous. But don't let that frighten you off, because armed with a good wild food guide you will very quickly have a vast free source of supply opened up to you.

One point we would make about wild food gathering though is the vital need to be on the lookout for possible pollution. There is one source, and one source only of pollution. Man. So gather your produce as far away from his activities as you possibly can. This is mainly a matter of common sense, but if you keep well away from road-side verges and any sort of habitation you should steer clear of trouble.

Commercial Supplies: The further you can get back along the chain of profit taking to the grower, the cheaper your raw materials are likely to be. Probably the cheapest source of supply will be a keen amateur grower—possibly with a road-side stall—who is not looking to make any great profits, but merely

to cover the cost of any materials and seed that he has had to buy in. In fact in times of real glut, food from such sources can often be entirely free. They will only be too glad for you to take it away. In many cases it will just be a matter of steeling your nerve and having the cheek to ask.

Another source of supply well back in the supply chain is the 'pick your own' farm. Because you are supplying the labour, the grower is able to keep his selling costs down to a minimum.

By the time the fruit and vegetables have reached the markets and shops, increased handling charges, profit taking, and wastage will have raised the prices dramatically. If this is your only source of supply, then all you can do is to pay up and try and get as good a price as you can by buying in bulk. But even buying at the top of the market you are still going to end up with 50% discount preserves. So if searching for supplies involves long trips away from home, you will probably be better off settling for the 'bargains' in the green-grocers around the corner.

The Preserving Year

The busiest time in the preserving year is in the late summer and autumn. The garden and hedgerow harvests will be groaning to be gathered, and the shops and markets positively bursting with produce in prime condition.

True enough it will be a time of concentrated effort for the dedicated home preserver, but this sudden burst of fertility will bring with it a

JAN   FEB   MAR   APRIL   MAY   JUNE   JULY   AUG   SEPT   OCT   NOV   DEC

Angelica
Apple
Apricot (fresh)
Apricot (dried)
Beetroot
Bilberry
Blackberry
Blackcurrant
Bullace
Carrot
Celery
Cherry
Chestnuts
Crab Apple
Cranberry
Cucumber
Damson
Elderberry
Elderflower
French Bean
Gooseberry
Grapefruit
Greengage
Haws
Lemon
Loganberry
Marrow
Mushroom
Nasturtium Seed
Nettle
Onion
Orange–Seville
Orange–sweet
Peach
Pear
Plum
Pumpkin
Quince
Raspberry
Red Cabbage
Redcurrant
Rhubarb
Rose hip
Rose petal
Rowanberry
Runner Bean
Shallots
Sloe
Strawberry
Tangerine
Tomato
Walnuts–pickling
Walnuts–salting

Chart showing when produce is in season.

number of advantages. Prices will be at their lowest, if produce must be bought. The bulk of the years work can be done in one fell swoop if you feel like it. And perhaps most important of all, you will be in the swing of things with all the various preserving techniques fresh in your mind.

The rest of the year will be a little less hectic; with perhaps the exception of the 'marmalade season' right at the beginning of the year.

But your preserving pan can be bubbling for 380 days of the year if you want. There will always be something to keep you busy if you feel like it. Crab Apple jelly and marrow chutney in November, or Nettle syrup and loganberry Jam in May. At any given time of the year one crop or the other will be in season.

On the other hand, the level of your involvement is entirely up to you. You can preserve as little or as much as you wish. You can bottle yourself into the ground, or dabble with just a few exotic specialities that appeal to you. The options are all yours. Whatever you want, whenever it suits you.

To help you with your decisions we have compiled the chart on the previous page. It shows when each crop can be expected to be ready for preserving. This will allow you to plan the whole of your preserving year well ahead. Or at least make sure that you don't miss out on the short season crops as they become briefly available.

Spices and Herbs

These form an important part of pickles, chutneys, sauces, some jellies and cheeses, and of course spiced vinegars. Their function, as in all cookery, being to add not only flavour or hotness, but often colour as well.

If you are reasonably active in the culinary arts already, you will probably have most of those that you will need, because none of the ones that appear in the following recipes are at all out of the way.

Here is a quick check list to help ensure that you are not caught out at a vital moment.

Nutmeg	Cloves
Mace	Ginger (ground &
Allspice	root)
Mixed Spice	Garlic
Paprika	Cayenne Pepper
Chilli's	Bay leaves
Mustard	Cinnamon
ground & seed)	Turmeric
Pepper	Salt

Sugar

In an emergency, fruit can be bottled quite acceptably without sugar, but its use does make for a better flavour, as well as helping to preserve colour and body. In fact under normal circumstances not using sugar in your processing can be something of a false economy. You will probably want to sweeten fruit when it arrives on the table anyway, and if it has not already taken up some from the modest amount used in the syrup, you will find you will have to add sugar regardless. So apart from anything else, you will be likely to find it cheaper to use sugar in the first place.

Sugar is used in most forms of preserving in this book—with the prominent exception of pickles—mainly as a flavourer. But in the case of jams and jellies (where large amounts are used) it assists the set and plays a dual role as a preservative as well.

Types of Sugar

Ordinary granulated sugar is the cheapest type to use. We find it absolutely satisfactory. The only snag is that it needs to be warmed before being added to jams and jellies or it will crystallize and cause a bit of a disaster. Special preserving sugar can be bought, but we find that its increased price outbalances that extra little bit of care that we have to take if we don't use it.

As a general rule, white sugar should be used, but where it will not adversely affect the colour (in chutney or a dark marmalade etc) brown sugar can be used for its flavour.

Always remember that brown sugar needs tamping down when used as a volume equivalent for white.

Honey

Honey can impart an interesting flavour to many preserves, and is well worth experimenting with. But remember it is powerful stuff. So select a fairly mild type, and use half the equivalent of sugar called for in the recipe. When weighing, icing sugar sprinkled on the scale pan will stop the honey sticking.

Pectin

Pectin is a natural gummy substance that causes jams, and other preserves to set. It is present to a greater or lesser extent in all fruit. But since the degree of its presence does vary, you will have to be aware of how much pectin is likely to be in your raw material or you may end up with sloshy un-set preserves.

Testing for Pectin Content

Some fruits have a high pectin content, and others very little at all. In a moment we will give you some specific examples, but since we can't list all the fruits you could possibly be using, we will outline a simple test that will allow you to pectin grade your own raw materials.

Add a teaspoon of the cooked fruit juice to three teaspoons of methylated spirit. If the fruit is high in pectin a firm lump of jelly will form. If very low in pectin, you will have created a mass of much smaller pieces. With fruit that has a medium content the result will be somewhere between the two and you will get three or four softish lumps.

To save you all the bother of testing the more common kinds of fruit, below are a few examples of fruits with high, medium, and low pectin contents:

High—Oranges, lemons, apples, plums, redcurrants, blackcurrants, and gooseberries.

Medium—Blackberries, raspberries, loganberries, and apricots.

Low—Strawberries, and cherries.

So, having established that you need a fairly high pectin content in order to get a good set, what do you do if this is not the case with the raw materials that you want to use? Well, there are a number of alternative solutions. You can cheat a bit and add a commercial pectin. You can add the juice of a high pectin fruit. Or you can do what most people do and mix a high pectin fruit in with the low one. Which, in case you had ever wondered, is why you get jams of seemingly strange combinations of fruit. Apple and blackberry, redcurrant and raspberry, and so on. Yet another solution is to add lemon juice. This is usually done when a mixture of fruit is not required—strawberry jam for example.

Water

In this country we are lucky in that our tap water is usually of the highest standard. So you should run into no problems in obtaining the sort of bacteria free supply that is an essential basic requirement of home preserving. Your only headache is liable to stem from the fact that you live in a 'hard water' area. This kind of water has a high mineral content—usually calcium—and it can cause discolouration, or shrivelled and toughened preserves. Happily, in all but a few areas, minerals will not be present in sufficient quantities to cause you trouble. But if you are unlucky, boil all water first—leave it to settle for half an hour—then pour it carefully off. This will leave the mineral salts safely deposited on the bottom of the pan.

Alternatively you could buy distilled water, but this would be an expensive way round the problem, and hardly in keeping with the money saving aspects of home preserving.

Types of Salt

As a general rule, it is safest always to use coarse cooking salt in home preserving. Ordinary table salt can be used in very small quantities just to add a touch of flavour; but the additives used to keep it free running (as well as the complication of filters) can affect the taste and colour or make the preserves go cloudy. Because of it s iodine content, Sea Salt can also cause problems. So if you want to play it absolutely safe, use coarse cooking salt right across the board. Not only will you be liable to get the best results, you will save money as well because its usually the cheapest of the lot.

Presentation

If you are thinking of either selling your preserves or entering local competitions with them, you will need to display their beauty to beholders in the best possible light. So below are a few tips that we hope will be of some help.

Now some people might argue that making any special concessions to visual appeal is to walk dangerously back near the doors of the supermarket, and the glossy packs of produce that look absolutely marvellous, but taste of nothing at all. Marginally, very marginally, they might have some sort of case, but not much of one. Because about the most heinous

concessions you will be making will be towards slightly more assiduous grading, and the use in some cases of storage mediums that are a little biased in favour of letting the dog see the rabbit. Handsome is as handsome does, and on that count home preserves will make any comparisons a no contest. All you are doing is taking a little more trouble than you normally would. Togging your efforts up in their Sunday best.

Processing for Appeal

In general, fruit and vegetables that are to retain their original shape to any extent should be of a uniform size. For competitions in particular, the more detailed the attention you pay to this point the greater your chances of success will be. Visual appeal is often the only aspect of your preserve that judges have a chance to evaluate.

Pickled Vegetables: These usually taste better when malt vinegar is used as the basis of the medium, but their quality can be better seen (and they photograph better if that matters) if a clearer white vinegar is used.

Bottled Fruit: Care with packing the jars is an important point here. And the use of a fairly light syrup that will allow the contents to be seen at their best and not force the fruit up towards the lid another.

Layer sliced fruit in imaginative patterns with the opened sides all facing outwards. A good tip in displaying peaches is to crack open the kernel and put the nut back in place. Or plug the gap with a grape. This always looks particularly attractive.

Packaging

From the point of view of competitions, the first thing to check on is whether there are any special rules about sizes of containers and labelling etc. Having won (purely because you have read this book) it will be infuriating to be disqualified because of some stupid piece of small print.

Labels and containers for other uses can be a more personal choice. But it is well worth taking some trouble with design. Perhaps even getting your local printer to run off a supply of labels to your own specifications. This will not cost the earth, and will certainly add an element of panache. If you consider the design carefully, you might also be able to use them as wine labels, book labels, and parcel labels etc. Which will at least give them alternative uses should your preserving enthusiasm ever wane.

One popular form of container decor is an outer lid covering of fabric; secured by a concealed elastic band or some type of ribbon. A circle of gingham is about the most popular, and one has to admit that it does carry with it a certain 'old fashioned country produce' sort of image. But it has been rather overdone, and it may well pay you to venture towards something a little more original.

Storage

Correct storage is a vital part of home preserving, for without it, your produce will quite simply go bad. For the moment we will just outline the general basic rules; but in the chapters on specific preserves we will give fuller details of any particular requirements.

The first thing to remember is that the storage temperature must be cool and equable. So that rules out hot steamy kitchens *and* most outhouses. We did say cool. Frost can do just as much damage to home preserves as a storecupboard next to the boiler would do.

Your store must also be dark. Sunlight will not only discolour your preserves, but could also cause them to ferment. And we don't want the vicar getting tipsy on your blackberry and apple jam do we?

Another important point is that your store must also be bone dry. Damp will encourage mould and fungal growth, which as we explained in the last chapter can also cause disaster. A further encouragement to unwanted growths is stagnant air—this and dampness often go hand in hand—so make sure that your store is also well ventilated.

Finally, a few points that are often overlooked. Firstly, make sure your storage containers are clean when you put them away. Jars dribbling jam are just an open invitation for destructive organisms to establish themselves. Secondly, always label your preserves. Not only with their date of manufacture and contents, but also with a consume by date. Then you will know exactly where you are.

Don't forget to occasionally turn out the contents of your store. Inspect each jar and bottle for signs of deterioration, and give each one a good dusting. Check also that no storage times are about to lapse. It is very easy to overlook the odd jar, especially if it contains something a little out of the ordinary that you would not be likely to eat every day of the week.

Equipment

Many of the recipes in this book can be tackled with the very minimum of equipment. To prove that, here is a list of the basic odds and ends that you can get by with. They will restrict you to the simplest forms of preserving it's true, but at least you will be able to make a start with practically no outlay at all.

Preserving pan and saucepans
Measuring jug
Wooden spoons
Scales
Sharp knives
Kitchen bowls
Muslin
Jam jars or coffee jars with plastic lids
Labels

Later on, we'll have a look at each of them in more detail, just to make sure that you have got *exactly* the right type. About the only things there are any doubts about finding in most modestly equipped of kitchens are—a preserving pan, some muslin, and labels.

Labels you can improvise, and muslin you can pick up on your next trip to the shops. As far as the preserving pan is concerned, well if you haven't got one and can't borrow one, then you will have to buy one. They are not expensive, but a decent one will last you a lifetime and pay for itself in no time at all. We will tell you exactly what type to buy in the glossary at the end of this chapter.

To cope with the full range of preserves that one is ever liable to consider making at home will require a more comprehensive range of equipment. Again you will probably have many of the items already, but even if you had to go out and buy everything from scratch it would not cost you a king's ransom.

Preserving pan and saucepans
Measuring jug
Scales
Sharp knives
Bowls
Muslin
Storage jars, jam, coffee, earthenware
Glass bottles
Large glass sweet jars
Mincer
Grater
Sieves and strainers
Wide necked funnel
Thermometer
Steriliser
Bottling jars (Kilner)
Jelly bag
Draining spoon
Asbestos mat
Paraffin wax
Jam pot covers and labels
Pressure cooker

With that lot you will be able to tackle just about everything. So let's have a look at them all in rather more detail, then we will be sure we are all talking about the same thing.

Asbestos mats: These are easily come by in kitchen shops and ironmongers. They are used to stand jars on in the oven during heat treatments.

Bowls: Made of ovenproof glass or china. Most kitchens already have a selection, but if you are thinking of preserving large amounts, you will need one or two jumbo sized ones.

Measuring jug: An ordinary heatproof glass one pint measuring jug.

Wooden spoons: A selection of various shapes and sizes is always useful, but for preserving they will need to have extra long handles because sometimes constant stirring may be involved and you will need to keep away from the heat.

Scales: Just about any sort that work. And that seems to be too much to ask of many that are on sale nowadays. A good old fashioned set with separate weights is the best in our opinion.

Sharp knives: You need two basically. A short bladed 4 or 5 inch general purpose knife and a longer 9 or 10 inch chopping knife.

Muslin: This can sometimes take a bit of tracking down. You can get by with a metre or so, but once you have found a stockist it will be just as well to get in two or three times that amount. It is used for straining purposes mainly.

Jelly bag: These can be bought in kitchen supply shops and are just made up bags for straining jellies and syrups etc. You can manage perfectly well without them by just using ordinary lengths of muslin. But if you can afford them, they will probably make things easier for you.

Mincer: These are helpful in preserving, and of course have many other uses as well. The modern kitchen seems to have difficulty in providing a substantial 'bolting on' surface—but alternative free-standing models are available. The old fashioned type was of course originally designed to be fixed to the overhanging edge of the scrubbed top kitchen table.

Grater: This is used for grating orange and lemon peel etc., and for reducing the ingredients of chutneys. Any of the multi-surface hand graters will do, although the best seem to be of French origin.

Labels. Important that these stick well or the type of preserve and its bottling date may become a mystery.

Paraffin wax: Obtainable from ironmongers, it is used mainly for sealing sauce bottles.

Draining spoon: Basically a large serving spoon with large holes in it. These are often acquired in a set along with slices, ladles, vegetable mashers, and the odd item or two that look nice hanging on their bracket in the kitchen.

Funnels: You really need two plastic ones. A large one for general use, and a small one for pouring sauce into bottles etc.

Sieves & Strainers: These should be of nylon, and in many respects the finer the mesh the better. See what you can find on offer, and if you can afford it buy a varied selection of each—they are always useful.

Thermometers: A cooking thermometer is not essential in home preserving, but it is a help. So if you have often toyed with the idea of buying one, but never actually got round to it, now will be as good a time as any to take the plunge. But as we say, thermometers are certainly not obligatory, and when the need arises we shall be teaching you the tricks of the trade, or giving alternative methods that will allow you to manage perfectly well without one.

Jam pot covers: These usually come in packs of either a small or a large size. Included are waxed paper discs, cellophane covers, bands and sometimes labels as well.

Pressure cookers: Can speed everything up and probably save fuel as well. Makers specifications will say if they are suitable for preserving, but if buying, make sure they are deep enough to take your jars.

Saucepans: The normal selection of saucepans, but preferably thick bottomed to prevent burning.

Double saucepan: Very useful in home preserving, and in many other forms of cooking as well. A bowl over a pan of water is a very practical alternative though.

Bottling jars: Various makes in various sizes are on the market, but screw top Kilner—the type we use—are probably the most widely available. One pound and two pound sizes are about the most useful.

Storage jars: Old jam jars, plastic screw top coffee jars, glass bottles, glazed earthenware crocks, large glass sweet jars—you name it. If you have ever worried that it seems a tragedy that so many glass containers are doomed to a one cycle existence, now is your chance to do something about it. Hoard them—you can never have enough.

Preserving pans: These come in various sizes, and for the keen home preserver the bigger the better. But remember it has to fit on your stove! A good average size to kick off with is a 12"—2 gallon aluminium one. You can manage with large saucepans of course, but the bucket handles and pouring lips of a proper pan make life much easier. Old fashioned preserving pans made of brass, copper, or brass, are best avoided as reactions with these metals during processing—except in jam making—can produce undesirable effects.

Weights and Measures

We give two sets of measurements in our recipes. Standard Imperial and Metric. The important thing to remember is that the equivalents are not exact, and so the quantities are not interchangeable between the two scales. So stick to either one set or the other all the way through a recipe and you will not go far wrong.

Bottling

Bottling

The art of preserving fruit by bottling is a traditional one and easy to do with the right equipment. At one time it was practised only by farmer's wives, but with the advent of the economies of World War Two, many other housewives were persuaded to have a go. Once the equipment was bought, and the mystery of bottling explained, it became an annual event.

Even if you have a freezer, it is a good idea to bottle fruit, because it leaves valuable space for meats, fish, and other produce. Bottled fruits are delicious in pies or puddings, or served on their own with custards, ice cream, or junkets.

The basic procedure is to sterilize the fruit and its container, and then seal it by heat treatment to exclude bacteria-ridden air. There is a cold water bottling method, which we will explain, but it is not so widely used as the preserves will not keep so long as those treated with heat.

Jam can also be made from bottled fruit—although the setting qualities will not be so good. However, this can be rectified by adding extra pectin to help the set along.

Vegetables can be bottled as well as fruit, but because of the problems involved with their low acid content the results are often disappointing.

Types of Jar

There are two sorts of vacuum jars; one secured with a screw band, and the other with a clip. Both types have metal or glass lids, with rubber rings to separate the lids from the bottles. Lacquered metal lids with the rubber ring already attached can now be bought, and they are easy to use as well as being great time savers.

Once the special jars are acquired, they can be used again and again, with only the clips and the rubber rings needing replacement from time to time.

Equipment

There are various methods of processing bottles, and we will explain all of them in detail. But the equipment required varies with the particular method.

Oven methods: For these you will need a baking sheet, wooden board, or asbestos mat.

Alternatively you can use some sort of suitable cardboard, or a thick layer of newspaper.

Water Bath methods: For these you will need a deep, covered saucepan. And something to stand the jars on inside the pan. A proper trivet is the best thing, but you can get away with a thick cloth or towel, or even a wad of newspaper. A thermometer is essential for the slow bath method.

Pressure Cooker method: A pressure cooker! And a trivet.

If there are any particular manufacturer's instructions for using their bottles, make sure that you familiarize yourself with them before you start. The rules for bottling are critical, and their observation, together with the correct equipment is vital.

The Raw Materials

Fruit: All fruit should be firm and ripe, and any damaged bits or bruises cut out. Some fruits are more successful than others, but expertise can help things along. Small soft berries should not be tightly packed as this makes them difficult to sterilize. Pears can lose their colour, so add some lemon peel to the syrup.

All fruit can be cooked to a pulp before bottling, to be served later as a dessert or whatever. This is particularly useful since you will then be able to produce apple sauce at the drop of a hat.

Syrup

Water or syrup can be used, but a better flavour and colour is achieved with syrup; and anyway, as we explained earlier, bottling fruit in plain water can be something of a false economy. You often end up having to add far more in the end than you would have done if you'd added sugar in the first place.

Heavy, medium, or light syrups can be made by adding 8, 6, or 4 ozs of sugar to 1 pt of water. (250, 175, or 125g to 600ml). Golden syrup or honey can be substituted for the sugar, but will give a different flavour and colour. A heavy syrup can cause certain fruits to rise in the bottle, so use a medium sweetness if you are in any doubt.

Spices, citrus fruit rinds, spirits or liqueurs can be added to the syrup for extra flavour.

Making Syrup

To make the syrup, dissolve the sugar in the

water over a gentle heat. Add any flavourings, and then bring to the boil and simmer for 2 minutes.

Filling the Bottles

Wash and prepare the chosen fruit. Apples and pears should be peeled, cored, and sliced. Then immersed immediately into a solution of water and lemon juice to prevent discolouration. Drain before packing into jars. Gooseberries should be topped and tailed, and currants stripped from their stalks. Peaches are usually cut in halves and stoned. While other stone fruits such as plums, damsons, and apricots are often bottled whole. But they can be halved and stoned like peaches if you prefer.

Remove the hulls (the little green star fish shaped leaves) from raspberries, loganberries, and blackberries, and cut rhubarb into even lengths.

Pack the fruit into the prepared wet jars, being careful not to bruise the fruit. Use a wooden spoon to help press the fruit down gently. Avoid leaving any large gaps between the fruits. Fill to within ½"—1" from the top.

Pour the hot or cold syrup—depending on the method used—onto the fruit. Then gently tap the sides of the jars to make any air bubbles rise to the surface.

Testing the Seal

As the processed bottles cool, tighten the screwbands every now and again. Leave to stand for 24 hours. Then take off the screwband, or clip, and carefully lift each bottle by the lid. If the seal is successful, the lid will stay on and a vacuum has formed. If the lid comes away from the jar, you have a failure, so the contents must be used up within a few days. There is no need to replace the screwbands, but we do, otherwise we find that we forget where they are! Lightly grease the bands with oil before replacing.

Storing Bottles

Wipe and label filled and processed bottles and put into a cool, dark storecupboard.

When wanted for use, take off the lid by inserting the point of a knife in between the rubber ring and the lid. and gently lever off. Discard any rubber rings that are not perfect.

To store empty bottles, wash them thoroughly and grease the screwbands to prevent rust. Any remaining rubber rings can be kept supple by sprinkling them with a little talcum powder.

The Processing Methods

The Slow Oven

This is perhaps the easiest method and requires the least equipment. The fruit does tend to shrink, so process a topping up jar along with the others. Pack the fruit into the warmed jars. Do not add syrup at this stage. Put the packed jars on a wooden board, asbestos mat, or a folded newspaper, and cover them with a baking sheet. Pre-heat the oven to 120°C/250°F or Gas mark ½. Leave the jars in the oven for ¾hr—1½hrs depending on the type of fruit.

Timetable

Raspberries, loganberries, currants blackberries	45 mins
Rhubarb, gooseberries	50 mins
Apples, plums, cherries, and damsons	1 hr
Apricots, peaches, pears	1¼ hrs
Tomatoes	1½ hrs

These times are for quantities up to 4 lbs (2 kgs). Add on 5—10 minutes for larger amounts.

Adding the Syrup & Closing the Jars

Have the cleaned lids, rubber rings, clips and screw bands ready (if clips are being used), as well as the pan of boiling syrup.

Lift the jars out of the oven with a pair of tongs or an oven mitt. Put on a dry surface, preferably wooden (so that the jars won't crack), and top up with spare fruit from the extra jar if necessary. Immediately fill each jar to overflowing with the boiling syrup. Put on the rubber rings, lids, clips or screw bands.

As the jars cool, tighten the screw bands. Leave until next day, then test for seal, wipe well, label, and store.

Moderate Oven Method

This is a better oven method to use for apples, apricots, peaches, pears, and plums. The syrup is added before they go into the oven, and so they do not discolour so much.

Pack the warmed jars with the prepared fruit. Then pour on the boiling syrup to within 1″ of the brim.

Only put on the rubber rings and lids, not the bands or clips.

Space the jars 2″ apart on an asbestos mat or a baking sheet covered with cardboard or newspaper. Then place in a preheated oven, 150 C/300 F or gas mark 2. Leave in the oven for the times already given for the slow oven method, but deduct 15 minutes for each fruit.

Slow Water Bath Method

Pack the fruit into warmed jars. Top up with COLD syrup or water, making sure that there are no air bubbles. Put on the rubber rings, lids, clips, or screw bands. Tighten the bands, then unscrew them a quarter turn. Place a trivet, thick cloth or towel in the base of a deep saucepan, and put in the bottles making sure they are not touching. To be sure, place pieces of cardboard between each jar. Cover with cold water and put the lid on the pan.

Heat the water gently, gradually bringing it to simmering point, 79.5 C/175 F in 1½ hours. Using a thermometer, keep at this temperature for 10 minutes, except for very large fruits which must be maintained at a temperature of 88 C/190 F for 30 minutes.

Take out the jars with tongs, or bale out enough water to use an oven mitt or cloth. Put onto a wooden surface, and tighten the screw bands. Leave to get cold, tightening the screw bands as they cool. Then next day, test for seal, wipe, label, and store.

Fast Water Bath Method

A thermometer is not necessary for this

method, and hot syrup is used to pour onto the fruit before it is heat treated.

Pack the prepared fruit into warmed jars. Fill up with hot syrup, and cover the jars as for the slow water bath method. Immerse the bottles in a deep pan containing hand-hot water. Bring to simmering point in 30 minutes and maintain for 2—40 minutes, depending on the fruit.

Timetable

Sliced apples, blackberries, currants, gooseberries, loganberries, raspberries, rhubarb, and strawberries.	2 mins
Apricots, cherries, damsons, whole plums	10 mins
Peaches, halved plums	20 mins
Pears, whole tomatoes	40 mins

Finish the process as for the slow water bath method.

If you are wondering why halved plums should be cooked longer than whole plums—which on the face of it seems illogical—it is simply because you get more halved plums in the jar, and have more of a solid mass to be cooked through.

Pressure Cooker Method

This method can be used if your pressure cooker is deep enough to take a trivet and the bottles standing on it. Your cooker also has to be able to maintain a low steady pressure—5 lbs per sq. inch.

You may have the manufacturers instructions for bottling with your pressure cooker, if not, use the following guide.

Preparation

Pack the prepared fruit into warm bottles, top up to within ½″ of the brim with boiling syrup. Put on the rubber rings, lids, clips or screwbands. Tighten the screw bands, then loosen them a quarter turn.

Place a trivet in the base of the pressure cooker, and add about 1″ of boiling water. Put in the bottles, separating them with a cloth or pieces of cardboard.

The Heat Treatment

Put the lid on the cooker and heat slowly, leaving the vent open until the steam is streaming out in a steady jet.

Close the vent to 5 lbs per sq. in. pressure. This should take about 8 minutes.

Hold at this pressure for 2 minutes for apples and all soft fruits. 4 minutes for peaches, plums and greengages, and 5 minutes for pears and tomatoes.

Take the cooker off the heat. Leave to cool without opening the vent for at least 15 minutes. Lift the jars out onto a wooden surface, and immediately tighten the screw bands. Test for seal after 24 hours.

Wipe, label, and store.

Bottling Fruit Pulp

Do not use over-ripe fruit as this could cause fermentation. Any damaged or bruised parts of the fruit must be cut out.

Prepare the fruit as you would for stewing. Put in a saucepan with barely enough water to cover, and sugar to taste. Simmer to a pulp.

Have ready the scalded jars, lids and rubber

rings. Pour the boiling pulp into the hot jars, put on the rubber rings, lids, clips and screw bands. Unscrew the bands a quarter turn. Put the jars into a pan of nearly boiling water, bring to the boil and keep at boiling point for 5 minutes. Take out and proceed as for the Fast Water Bath Method.

Bottling Tomato Puree

Choose ripe, completely red tomatoes. There is no need to skin them.

Make a brine solution of 1 oz (25 g) salt to 2 pts (1.21) water. Put the tomatoes in a pan and pour in enough brine to come half way up the tomatoes. Cook until soft then rub them through a nylon or hair sieve.

Return the puree to the pan and reheat until just boiling. Pour immediately into hot jars and continue as for fruit pulp, but allow 8 minutes boiling instead of 5 minutes.

Bottled Tomatoes

Wash the tomatoes and pack tightly into prepared jars, sprinkling on a very little sugar between each layer. Fill the bottles with a hot or cold brine solution, (depending on the method used) of 1 oz (25 g) salt to 2 pts (1.2 l) water.

Continue bottling with the Moderate oven method, water bath methods or Pressure cooker. The times for tomatoes are given with each method.

Bottled Fruit Salad

Choose a combination of fruits, remembering that dark fruits will colour the lighter ones.

Make a heavy syrup with 1 lb (500g) sugar, 1 pt (600m) water, the grated rind and juice of a large lemon, and a few drops of angostura bitters if you have it. Bring these ingredients to the boil slowly to dissolve the sugar, and boil for 2 minutes.

Prepare the fruits, tossing ones which are likely to go brown in lemon juice. Pack into prepared warm bottles, pour on the boiling syrup and continue with the moderate oven method, leaving the jars in the oven for 45 minutes.

Bottling Fruit in Brandy

Bottled fruit in brandy is very expensive, so it is well worth doing some to keep for a treat at Christmas.

Peaches, apricots, pears and raspberries are ideal fruits to bottle in this way.

Prepare the fruit in the normal way, pricking any tough skinned fruits five or six times with a needle, so that the brandy flavour penetrates the fruit.

Make a heavy syrup, allow to cool, and for each 1 pt (600m) syrup add ¼ pt 150m) brandy.

Pack the fruit into the jars, pour on the cold syrup and proceed with the slow water bath method. If preferred, use the slow oven method, packing the fruit into the jars, but pouring on the boiling syrup after the jars have been taken from the oven.

Cold Water Bottling

This is a little heard of way of preserving high-acid fruits like gooseberries and lemons. Or if you happen to have a supply of any, cranberries as well. No heat is used in the process, so it is very economical—but obviously the end product will not keep as long as fruit sterilized in the normal way.

Choose only gooseberries and lemons that are in first class condition. Firm fruit with tough skins and no blemishes. This is vital.

Method

Sterilize the jars and utensils in the normal way and allow them to cool. Wash the fruit carefully and well and place it in the jars. Slowly fill the jars to the brim with cold running water, and then place them in a deep sterilized container. This container or pan has to be deep enough to totally submerge the jars. Now fill this container with running water until the tops of the jars are well below the surface level. Then with the jars still under water secure their lids.

Store in a cool dark place, but do not freeze.

We think that this is a particularly good way of keeping a few lemons handy for all those times you could really do with some but forgot to get any in. In this country, lemons seem to maintain a fairly standard price all the year round—so it will be no real economy to preserve them. But as we say, this is one way of always having some in stock.

Conserves and Syrups

Conserves and Syrups

Conserves

Conserves are an easy method of preserving whole or sliced fruit, but they do not keep for so long as special bottles are not used.

These days, many shop bought jams are labelled conserves, but true conserves differ from jams in that they do not set as firmly, and are used for desserts rather than for spreading.

Equipment

Only a few items of equipment are needed. Scales, a bowl, a large saucepan or preserving pan, clean jam jars and covers. A draining spoon and funnel is useful, but not essential.

The Principle

A conserve is made by layering the prepared fruit with sugar overnight. This extracts the natural juices from the fruit, and toughens the skins to hold the shape of the fruit whilst cooking.

The fruit and sugar are simmered with the natural juices until the fruits are tender, but still retain their shape.

They are used principally as desserts.

Storing

Jars of conserves should be labelled with the contents and date and stored in a cool dark cupboard. Check regularly for deterioration as they do not keep as long as jam or bottled fruit.

Strawberry Conserve

3 lbs (1.5 kg) strawberries
3 lbs (1.5 kg) sugar
Grated rind and juice of 3 lemons

Hull the strawberries, and layer them with the sugar in a bowl. Leave to stand overnight in a warm place to extract the juice. Strain the fruit, and put the juice and sugar in a large pan. Heat gently until the sugar is dissolved, then bring to the boil. Continue boiling until the juice is the consistency of thick syrup, about 30 minutes. Add the strawberries, grated rind and juice of the lemons, and simmer gently until the fruit is tender, about 5 minutes. Cool before potting.

Rhubarb and Orange Conserve

4 lbs (2 kg) rhubarb
4 oranges
4 lbs (2 kg) sugar
2 ozs (50 gm) split almonds
1 oz (25 gm) root ginger

Cut the rhubarb into ½ inch slices and put in layers with the sugar in a large bowl. Cover and leave overnight to extract the juice. Strain and reserve the rhubarb. Put the juice and sugar in a pan. Grate the oranges, cut away the pith with a sharp knife, and remove the pips. Tie the pith, pips and peeled and chopped root ginger in a muslin bag. Cut the orange flesh into segments. Put the muslin bag in the pan with the juice and sugar, heat gently, stirring, and when dissolved, bring to the boil. Boil rapidly for 15 minutes, then add the rhubarb, orange and almonds. Continue simmering gently for a further 15 minutes. Remove the muslin bag and cool completely before potting.

Apricot Conserve

3 lbs (1.5 kg) apricots
3 lbs (1.5 kg) sugar
2 pts (1.2 litres) water

First make a syrup by dissolving 1¼ lbs (625 gm) sugar in the 2 pts (1.2 litres) water over a gentle heat, then boiling for 10—15 minutes. Skin the apricots, remove the stones, and cut into halves. Put the fruit into the syrup and cook very gently until just tender. Cool at once by standing the pan in cold water. Leave covered overnight. Next day, add a further ¾

lb (350 gm) sugar, heat gently till dissolved, then boil for only 2 minutes. Leave to stand again overnight. Add the rest of the sugar, dissolve, and boil for 2 minutes. Cool until a skin forms, stir carefully, pot into hot jars and seal. This method may also be used for peaches, pineapples, plums and greengages.

Cherry Conserve

4 lbs (2 kg) cherries
3 lbs (1.5 kg) sugar
3 lemons

Stone the cherries. Crack open some of the stones and blanch and skin the kernels. Put the cherries, kernels and sugar in layers in a covered bowl and leave overnight. Next day, pour all the contents of the bowl into a large pan and add the grated rind and juice of the lemons. Put the lemon pips and pith in a muslin bag and add to the pan. Heat gently, stirring, and when the sugar is dissolved, bring to the boil and simmer for about 30 minutes, or until the fruit is tender and the syrup is thick. Remove the muslin bag, cool, pot and cover.

Mock Preserved Ginger

1 medium sized marrow
1 lb (500 gm) loaf sugar
½ pt (300 ml) water
1 oz root ginger

Peel the marrow, remove the seeds and cut into large cubes. Bruise the ginger. Put the sugar and water into a pan and stir over a gentle heat until the sugar has dissolved. Bring to the boil and continue boiling until the liquid is the consistency of thick syrup. Put in the cubes of marrow and the ginger. Remove from the heat when the cubes of marrow look clear. Pour carefully into a basin, cover and leave overnight. Next day, strain and return the liquid to a pan. Bring the syrup to the boil again until thick. Add the ginger and marrow and simmer for an hour. Put back into the basin and next day repeat the process. Take out the marrow with a draining spoon and put into jars. Pour over the syrup and cover.

Cooking apples may be used instead of marrow.

Apple Ginger Conserve

3 lbs (1.5 kg) cooking apples
2 lemons
3 lbs (1.5 kg) sugar
½ pt (300 ml) water
1 oz (25 gm) root ginger
4 ozs (125 gm) crystallized ginger

Peel and core the apples and put them in a solution of water and lemon juice to stop them going brown. Put the cores and peel with the ½ pt (300 ml) water in a pan, and simmer until the skins are soft. Strain. Thinly peel the lemons. Bruise the root ginger and tie with the peel in a muslin bag. Slice the apples and put them in a pan with the sugar, muslin bag and the strained water. Heat gently and when the sugar is dissolved, continue cooking until the apples are transparent and the syrup is thick. Remove the muslin bag, stir in the chopped crystallized ginger, pot and cover.

Peaches in Brandy

2 lbs (1 kg) peaches
8 ozs (250 gm) sugar
Brandy

Skin and stone the peaches, and cut into even slices. Put the peaches and sugar in layers in a large jar and pour over the brandy. Cover and place the jar in a saucepan of boiling water. Bring the brandy to simmering point, but do not let it boil. Remove from the heat, spoon the peaches into smaller jars and cover with the brandy and seal. This recipe may also be used for apricots.

A More Economical Peaches in Brandy

1 lb (500 gm) peaches
12 ozs (350 gm) sugar
½ pt (300 ml) water
Brandy

Do not skin the peaches but remove the hairs with a damp cloth. Put the sugar and water in a pan, heat gently stirring until the sugar has dissolved, then boil without stirring for 10 minutes. Add the peaches to the syrup and simmer until tender, about 5 minutes. Turn the peaches occasionally while cooking if they are not covered with the syrup. Take out the peaches with a draining spoon and pack into jars. Boil the syrup for a further 5 minutes, then measure it and add the same amount of brandy. Put the syrup and brandy back into the pan and bring to the boil. Pour over the peaches and cover.

Syrups

Syrups are a concentrated extraction of ripe fruit juices with added sugar. Because of the large amount of sugar, they will keep longer than juices just sweetened with sugar, provided they are stored in sterilized bottles.

Syrups are delicious with water, soda, or milk, as drinks. They can also be used as sauces for puddings and ice creams, or for making jellies.

Equipment

Small screw top bottles are easy to use and sterilize, but bottles with corks sealed with melted paraffin wax are an alternative.

The other equipment needed is scales, a large bowl, suitable saucepan, a fine nylon sieve, and a pouring jug. You will also need a fruit squeezer, and grater or jelly bag for some of the recipes. A funnel and a thermometer will also be useful, but are not essential.

Sterilizing and Filling the Bottles

The bottles, tops or corks should be sterilized before the syrups are poured in. Then sterilized again afterwards, and finally sealed.

To sterilize the empty bottles, put them in a pan of water together with the tops or corks, bring to the boil, and simmer for 10 minutes.

When filling the bottles, leave a 1" space at the top of a screw top bottle and 1½" for corked bottles.

To sterilize after the syrups have been put in the bottles, stand them on a trivet or thick cloth in a deep pan, with cardboard or cloth separating the bottles. Fill the pan with cold water up to the necks of the bottles. Bring the water slowly to simmering point, 88°C/190°F, and maintain at this temperature for 20 minutes. A thermometer is useful here, but not essential.

Remove the bottles and put on the screw tops or corks. If using corks, dip them in melted paraffin wax when they are cold.

Chemical Sterilizing

An alternative method of sterilizing is to add a crushed campden tablet (Sulpher dioxide), dissolved in 1 tablespoon of warm water, to the syrup before pouring into the bottles. But we don't like this method because it discolours the syrup and gives a slight sulphur flavour, which although not poisonous (as far as we know), is rather off putting.

Storing

Label the bottles, and store in a cool, dark cupboard. The bottles can be put into brown paper bags to help preserve the colour if your store is not particularly dark.

Syrups should keep for at least 6 months if the processing has been carried out to the letter, and well fitting tops or corks used.

Once opened, the syrup should be used up within a week.

Nettle Syrup

1 lb (500 gm) tender, young nettle tops
1½ pts (900 ml) water
White sugar

Wash and drain the nettle tops and simmer with the water in a pan for an hour. Strain through a fine sieve. Measure the liquid, and to each pint add 1 lb of sugar (750 gm to 1 litre). Return to the pan, stirring until the sugar is dissolved, then simmer for 5 minutes. Pour into bottles, sterilize and seal.

This delicious old recipe is especially good when diluted with soda water, and is said to purify the blood.

Rose Hip Syrup

2 lbs (1 kg) fresh, ripe rose-hips
4½ pts (2.5 litres) water
1 lb (500 gm) sugar

Wash the hips and remove the stalks and calyces. Crush, grate or mince them. Bring 3 pts (1.8 litres) of the water to the boil and add the crushed rose-hips. Bring back to the boil then remove from the heat and allow to stand for 15 minutes. Strain through a jelly bag, extracting as much juice as possible. Bring the remaining 1½ pts (900 ml) of water to the boil and return the pulp to the pan. Re-boil and allow to stand as before. Strain in a clean jelly bag. Mix the two batches of juices, pour into a clean pan and boil until reduced to about 1½ pts (900 ml). Add 1 lb (500 gm) sugar. Stir over gentle heat until the sugar dissolves then boil for 5 minutes. Pour into clean warm bottles, sterilize and seal.

Elderberry or Blackberry Syrup

1 lb (500 gm) elderberries or blackberries
1 lb (500 gm) sugar
¼ pt (150 ml) water

Strip the elderberries from the stalks. Wash the fruit and put into a double saucepan with

the sugar and water. Cook gently, uncovered, for about 2 hours or until the liquid becomes syrupy. Stir often during cooking. Strain and pour into bottles, sterilize and seal. If you have it, a wineglass of brandy added to the syrup just before bottling improves the flavour!

Lemon Syrup

6 large lemons
1½ lbs (750 gm) white sugar
1½ pts (900 ml) water
1 tablesp. citric acid

Wash the lemons, grate the rinds and squeeze out the juice. Pour the juice into a large bowl. Put the rinds, sugar and water into a saucepan and heat gently, stirring, until the sugar has dissolved. Pour onto the juice and add the citric acid. Stir well then leave overnight. Next day, strain into bottles, seal and sterilize. This recipe can be used with oranges or grapefruit instead of lemons, but add the grated rind and juice of 1 lemon.

Strawberry Syrup

Raspberries or loganberries can be used instead of strawberries
4 lbs (2 kg) strawberries
Sugar
Lemon juice

Put the prepared berries into a large bowl and crush well. Either cover and leave overnight, or to speed the process, stand the bowl over a saucepan of boiling water and stir and crush the berries until the juice flows. Strain through a jelly bag, extracting as much juice as possible. Measure the juice, and to each pint (600 ml) add 12 ozs (350 gm) sugar and 1 tsp lemon juice. Heat very gently and remove from the heat as soon as the sugar has dissolved. Bottle, sterilize and seal.

Blackcurrant or red currant syrup may be made in this way, but add ½ pt (300 ml) water before crushing the berries, and cook the fruit in a saucepan instead of in a bowl over boiling water.

Elder Rob A Cure for Coughs and Colds

Elderberries
Demerara sugar
Cloves and cinnamon

Put the prepared elderberries into an ovenproof dish and cook in a moderate oven until the juice runs. Strain through muslin. To each pint (600 ml) add 12 ozs (350 gm) sugar, ½ tsp cinnamon and 10 cloves. Simmer for about 30 minutes, until thick. Strain and bottle when cold.

Jams, Jellies
and
Marmalades

Jams, Jellies & Marmalades

Jams

Jams are probably the best known preserves, storing well they can provide tasty reminders of hot summer days all the year round. Very often though, your jam making will be more successful after an indifferent summer than after a hot one. Too much sun will over-ripen the fruit, resulting in a poor set and less flavour. Jams can be made at any time of the year though, so if you are running out of your summer fruit jams, there are other recipes to make to fill the space in your storecupboard.

Apart from spreading on bread and butter, jams have many uses. In puddings, tarts, sponges, or even in sauces. Some also go well with meats.

All jams are easy to make once the basic principles are understood. So you must have clear in your mind such basics as how to establish pectin contents and be able to test for the set etc. For more detailed information—which fruits contain most pectin, and how to overcome the problem of a low pectin content etc. turn to Chapter 3.

Fruit

Choose fresh, ripe, or slightly under-ripe fruit. Over-ripe fruit will have lost some of it's pectin content. Wash and drain all fruits. Prepare the fruits for cooking, according to type. Remove stalks, peel, stones and cores.

Sugar

Preserving, lump, granulated, or caster sugar can be used. Preserving sugar costs more than granulated, but it does dissolve quicker, and helps prevent scum forming on the jam. Brown sugar can be used, but it will affect the flavour and colour of the jam. Always warm the sugar before stirring it into the fruit. It will dissolve quicker, and will not cool the jam.

For every 1 lb (500 gm) of sugar used, the yield of jam should be about 1⅓ lbs (650 gm). The quantity of sugar used is important for setting and keeping qualities—so do not experiment with them.

Method

The basic method for making jam is to soften the prepared fruits (with water if needed) by simmering. Any setting agents are then added, before the warmed sugar, which is then stirred over a low heat until it has dissolved. It is important to dissolve the sugar completely before bringing it to the boil, or it will crystallize and ruin the whole thing.

The jam is then boiled rapidly, stirring only occasionally to prevent it sticking to the bottom of the pan and burning.

Test for setting point after 3–20 minutes— depending on the type of fruit used. Avoid over-boiling, as this will spoil the colour and flavour of the jam. If there is a lot of scum on the jam, skim it off towards the end of the cooking process, or stir in a knob of butter.

Testing for Setting

An indication that setting point has been reached is when the jam makes heavy, plopping noises, and the rapid frothing has ceased. Turn off the heat before doing a setting test, or you may be over-boiling the jam whilst you are doing the test.

If you have a sugar thermometer, dip it in hot water before putting it in the jam, and then stir the jam with it for a few moments. If the temperature reaches 105 C/220 F the jam should have reached setting point.

If you don't have a thermometer, the jam is just as easily tested with a saucer or a wooden spoon. To test on the saucer, spoon a little jam onto a cold one and leave to cool. For quickness pop the saucer in the fridge. A skin will form on the jam which will wrinkle when pushed with the fingertip if it has reached setting point.

To test with a wooden spoon, stir the jam with it, and twist it around gently until the jam has cooled. If the jam has set, it will thicken on the spoon and the drops will run together to form large flakes when the spoon is turned on its side. If the flakes drop off the spoon quickly, the jam has not reached setting point.

Potting and Covering

Pour the jam immediately into clean, dry, warm jars, unless you are making a whole fruit jam, which should be allowed to cool for 10– 15 minutes, then stirred before potting to distribute the fruit evenly.

Fill nearly to the top of the jars, because the jam will shrink slightly on cooling. Cover the jam immediately with waxed paper discs (waxed side down), smoothing the surface to remove any air pockets.

Wipe the jars with a clean cloth wrung out in very hot water. Cover at once with the cellophane covers secured with rubber bands, or with metal or plastic screw top lids. Alternatively, let the preserves get completely cold before putting on the lids. They must be covered either hot or cold—not just in between and warm—or you will encourage mould.

Storage

Jams will keep for a very long time if properly stored in a cool, dry, dark place.

Things That May Go Wrong

Mould can form on top of the jam if there is

insufficient cooking of the fruit before the sugar is added, or if cold, wet jars are used for potting. Inadequate sealing and covering, and storage in a warm place can also have a similar effect. You can at a pinch eat jam that has gone a little mouldy—of course after you have removed the mould. But it should not have been stored for any length of time, because moulds obtain their sustenance from the acid content of the fruit, so as they are growing they are diminishing this preservative element.

Crystallization may be caused by adding too much sugar, or boiling the jam before the sugar has dissolved. Stirring too much after adding the sugar can also have the same result.

Fermentation will take place if too little sugar is used, or if the jam is insufficiently boiled before potting. Storage in a warm place or in day light may also cause fermentation.

Jellies

Jellies make a delicious change from jams. The process is longer and the yield is smaller, so wild fruits, or a cheap supply of cultivated ones are ideal for jelly making. High pectin fruits are best, as only the juices are used.

Fruit

All fruit should be ripe, but under-ripe rather than over-ripe to get a good set. Fruit for jellies needs less preparation than for jams, as any fruit used is strained through a jelly bag after cooking.

Wash and drain all fruits, and cut out any damaged or bruised parts. Leave in any stalks, peel, stones or cores, as these are a valuable source of pectin, and improve the set of the jelly. Large or tough skinned fruits should be roughly chopped.

Sugar

Any sort of sugar may be used, as for jam.

Method

The prepared fruits are simmered in a preserving pan with water until they are soft and pulpy. Hard fruits will need more water, and a longer cooking time than soft, juicy fruits.

The pulp is then strained through a jelly bag—preferably overnight. The fruit must not be pressed through the jelly bag or disturbed, as this could make for a cloudy jelly.

The juice is then measured, and for every one pint (600 ml) juice, 1 lb (500 gm) sugar is generally added. This can vary slightly for some recipes. The juice is brought to the boil in a large, clean pan. The warmed sugar is then added, and stirred over a low heat until it has dissolved, then boiled rapidly until setting point. This should take from 3—15 minutes. Test for setting, and pot and cover as for jams.

Jellies should be skimmed before potting, and this must be done quickly before the jelly starts to set.

Marmalades

The process for making marmalade is very similar to that for making jam, but usually citrus fruits are used, and the peels are included to give texture and flavour. Because the peels are used, the cooking time is longer than for jams.

Even though most of the fruits for marmalade have to be bought in the shops, your marmalade will still only cost half the price of ready made. As for flavour—no contest.

Fruit

The best known of the citrus fruits for making marmalade are the bitter, Seville oranges, as they have a good flavour and give a very nice colour. These can only be bought in the shops in January and February—so be sure you don't miss them—if you are particularly busy at that time, they can be frozen until you have time to spare. Other citrus fruits are available all the year round, and provide an interesting variation of flavour.

There are also some excellent tinned varieties of marmalade pulp to buy, which if time is important, cuts out the job of shredding peel, and still saves you money.

All citrus fruits are high in pectin which is contained mainly in the pips and pith, so these must be used in marmalade making to ensure a good set.

Any fruits used must be in good condition—firm and only just ripe.

Sugar

The same rules apply as for jam.

Method

As the preparation of fruits for marmalade making is a lengthy process, it is a good idea to prepare them one day, leave them soaking overnight in the water they are to be cooked in, and to do the actual cooking the next day.

As a rule, the fruits are washed well, cut in halves, and the juices squeezed out and reserved. The pips are kept to put in a muslin bag, together with the pith if this is removed from the peel. Alternatively, the pith may be finely shredded together with the peel. For quickness, the peel can be minced rather than shredded, but this gives a coarser marmalade.

Sometimes the fruits are cooked whole until softened before being shredded.

Whichever method is used, the peel, pips, pith, juice, and flesh are all used.

To soften the peel and reduce the flesh to a pulp in the specified amount of water, takes at least one hour, or longer. The mixture in the pan should be reduced by at least a third before adding the sugar. A pressure cooker is useful here as the cooking time for softening the peel will be about 15 minutes, instead of one hour or more. The marmalade must be finished in an open pan though once the sugar has been added.

If a muslin bag is used, this is then removed—before adding the warmed sugar. The sugar must be dissolved over a gentle heat, before fast boiling without stirring—although the occasional stir to prevent burning will not do any harm.

To reach setting point will take from 15–40 minutes, depending on the recipe used and the quantity being processed. Turn off the heat when testing for set, as for jam. Overboiling will spoil the set and darken the marmalade.

Potting Covering and Storing

Remove any scum as soon as setting point is reached. Allow to cool for 10–15 minutes, then stir to distribute the peel evenly. Do not stir a jelly marmalade though.

Pot, cover, and store as for jams.

Equipment for Jams, Jellies and Marmalades

The most essential piece of equipment is a preserving pan, or a large heavy based saucepan. These can be of aluminium, stainless steel, copper, or brass. Whichever is used must be thoroughly clean, as well as heavy based to prevent sticking and burning of the preserve.

You will also need scales, a measuring jug, a long handled wooden spoon, and jam jars and covers. The covers can either be waxed paper discs and cellophane rounds, or plastic/metal air tight screw tops. Plus of course labels.

Once again, a funnel and thermometer are useful but not essential.

For making jellies, a jelly bag is essential. A bought one will be made of flannel or closely woven cotton. But you can make one with 2 or 3 layers of muslin cloth or cheesecloth, or from a square of cotton sheeting, or even a tea towel. Whichever material you use must

be thoroughly scalded in boiling water before use though.

To strain the fruit through the jelly bag, tie the four corners of the cloth securely to the legs of an upturned stool. Place a large bowl under the jelly bag to catch the juice as it drips through.

For marmalade you will also need a fruit squeezer and muslin. A pressure cooker and mincer would also be useful, but you can manage perfectly well without them.

Blackcurrant Jam

4 lbs (2 kg) blackcurrants
4 pts (2.25 litres) water
8 lbs (4 kg) sugar

Put the prepared currants and the water in a preserving pan and simmer until the fruit is soft, about 15–30 mins. Add the warmed sugar, stir gently until dissolved, then boil rapidly until set. Pot and cover. Yields about 10 lbs (4½ kg).

Black Jam

2 lbs (1 kg) blackberries
2 lbs (1 kg) elderberries
3 lbs (1.5 kg) sugar

Strip the elderberries from the stalks and start simmering in a preserving pan. Wash and add the blackberries, bring slowly to the boil and simmer for about 15 minutes or until the fruit is soft. Add the warmed sugar, stir until dissolved, then boil rapidly until setting point is reached, about 20 mins. Pour into hot jars and cover.

Quince Jam

4 lbs (2 kg) quinces
Water
Sugar
Juice of 2 lemons

Peel and chop the quinces into small cubes or grate on a coarse grater. Put into a pan, cover with water and simmer until soft, 30 mins–1 hr. Measure the pulp and to every pint allow 1 lb sugar, (600 ml to 500 gm). Return to the pan with the sugar and lemon juice. Stir until the sugar is dissolved, then boil rapidly until set, about 20 mins. Pour into hot jars and cover.

Hedgerow Jam 1

3 lbs (1.5 kg) sloes
2 lbs (1 kg) crab apples or cooking apples
1 lb (500 gm) blackberries
1 lb (500 gm) elderberries
1 pt (600 ml) water
Sugar

Wash the fruit well, and chop the apples. Put all the fruit and the water in a preserving pan, and cook until tender. Rub through a sieve and weigh the pulp. To each 1 pt (600 ml) of pulp add 1 lb (500 gm) sugar. Return the pulp to the pan with the sugar and stir over a low heat until the sugar has dissolved. Boil rapidly until setting point is reached, then pot and cover. Yields about 7 lbs (3.5 kg).

Hedgerow Jam 2

1 lb (500 gm) blackberries
1 lb (500 gm) elderberries
1 lb (500 gm) crab apples
8 oz (250 gm) sloes
8 oz (250 gm) rowanberries
8 oz (250 gm) haws
8 oz (250 gm) rose hips
Water
Sugar

Wash the fruit well, and chop the apples. Put all the fruit, except the elderberries, in a preserving pan and just enough water to cover, and cook until really tender. Sieve and weigh the pulp. Return the pulp to the pan with the elderberries and simmer for a further

20 minutes. Add 1 lb (500 gm) sugar, plus 1 lb (500 gm) sugar for each 1 pt (600 ml) pulp. Cook over a gentle heat, stirring, and when the sugar has dissolved, boil rapidly until setting point. Pour into hot jars, cover and label. Yields about 6 lbs (3 kg).

Dried Fruit Jam

1 lb (500 gm) mixed dried fruit (apples, pears, apricots, plums, prunes etc.)
2 pts (1.2 litres) water
2 lbs (1 kg) sugar
1 orange
1 lemon

Put the fruit in a bowl with the water and leave overnight to soften. Next day, remove any stones from the fruit and put the fruit and the liquid into a preserving pan. Grate the rinds of the orange and lemon and squeeze out the juice. Add to the pan and bring to the boil. Simmer until all the fruits are very soft, about 1 hour. Add the warmed sugar and stir over a low heat until the sugar has dissolved. Boil rapidly until setting point. Remove any scum, cool slightly before potting. Cover and label. Yields about 4 lbs (2 kg).

Bilberry Jam

1 lb (500 gm) bilberries
1 lb (500 gm) sugar

Put the bilberries in a bowl, cover with the sugar, and leave overnight. Pour the fruit and the juices into a preserving pan and heat gently, stirring until the sugar has dissolved. Bring to the boil and simmer until set. Pour into hot jars and cover.

Fresh Apricot Jam

2 lbs (1 kg) fresh apricots
Grated rind and juice of 1 lemon
½ pt (300 ml) water
2 lbs (1 kg) sugar

Wash the apricots, cut in half and remove the stones. Crack open half the stones with a hammer and remove the skins from the kernels. Tie the rest of the stones in a muslin bag. Put the apricots, kernels, lemon rind and juice with the water in a large pan and simmer gently until the fruit is tender, about 15 minutes. Add the warmed sugar, stir over a low heat until it has dissolved, then add the muslin bag. Boil rapidly until setting point is reached. Skim if necessary, cool for a few minutes then stir to distribute the fruit evenly. Pour into warm jars, cover and label. Yields about 3 lbs (1.50 kg).

Gooseberry Jam

3 lbs (1.5 kg) gooseberries
4 lbs (2 kg) sugar
1 pt (600 ml) water

Top and tail the gooseberries, wash and drain. Put into a preserving pan with the water and cook gently until pulpy. Add the warmed sugar, dissolve stirring, then boil rapidly until setting point. This should take about 15–20 minutes. Yields about 5 lbs (2.5 kg).

Cherry Jam

4 lbs (2 kg) cherries
3 lbs (1.5 kg) sugar
Juice of 2 lemons *or* 1 tsp citric acid

Stone the cherries and tie the stones in a muslin bag. Simmer the cherries in a very little water in a preserving pan with the muslin bag. When they are tender, remove the muslin bag, and add the lemon juice and the warmed sugar. When the sugar has dissolved, boil rapidly until setting point. Turn into hot jars and tie down. Yields about 5 lbs (2.5 kg).

Pineapple Jam

1 large or 2 small pineapples
Sugar
1 pt (600 ml) water
Grated rind and juice of 3 large lemons

Peel the pineapple and remove the hard centre core. Cut into slices and weigh. For each 1 lb (500 gm) flesh you will need 1 lb (500 gm) sugar. Cut the pineapple into small pieces, and put in a pan with the water, lemon rind and juice. Simmer until the pineapple is soft, about 20–30 minutes. Add the warmed sugar and stir till dissolved, then boil rapidly until setting point. Leave to stand for about 10 mins then pour into hot jars and cover. Yields about 4 lbs (2 kg).

Dried Apricot Jam

2 lbs (1 kg) dried apricots
1½ oz (40 gm) almonds
5½ lbs (2.75 kg) sugar
5½ pts (3.3 litres) water

Wash the apricots. Mince or cut them into small pieces. Soak overnight in the water. Next day put the apricots, water and sugar in a preserving pan and heat gently stirring, until the sugar has dissolved. Bring to the boil and

simmer for 30 minutes. Meanwhile, blanche and shred the almonds. Add them to the pan and continue simmering for a further 30 minutes, or until setting point is reached. Pour into hot jars, cover and label. Yields about 8 lbs (4 kg).

Whole Fruit Plum or Greengage Jam

2 lbs (1 kg) plums or greengages
2 lbs (1 kg) sugar

Wash the fruit and cut into halves. Crack open as many of the stones as you wish and add the kernels to the fruit. Put the fruit and the kernels into a bowl and sprinkle over the sugar. Leave overnight. Put all into a preserving pan and heat gently, stirring, until the sugar has dissolved. Boil rapidly until the fruit is soft and the jam has set, approx 15–20 minutes. Pour into hot jars, cover and label. Yields about 2½ lbs (1.25 kg).

Strawberry Jam

2 lbs (1 kg) strawberries
2 lbs (1 kg) sugar
Juice of 2 lemons

Simmer the strawberries until soft, then add the lemon juice and sugar and stir well until dissolved. Boil rapidly until set.

If a whole fruit jam is preferred, put the strawberries and the sugar into a pan, and heat together gently until the sugar has dissolved. Then add the lemon juice and boil steadily until set. Pot, cover and label. Yields about 2½ lbs (1.25 kg).

Rhubarb and Orange Jam

3 lbs (1.5 kg) rhubarb
1 lb (500 gm) oranges
3 lbs (1.5 kg) preserving or granulated sugar

Wash the rhubarb and cut up into small pieces. Spread in layers with the sugar in a bowl and leave to stand overnight. Boil the oranges whole in water until they are tender. Using a knife and fork, finely slice the oranges, removing the pips. Put the rhubarb and sugar in a preserving pan with the sliced oranges and heat gently until the sugar has dissolved. Bring to the boil and simmer until setting point. Remove any scum, cool slightly and pour into hot jars, cover and label. Yields about 4 lbs (2 kg).

Blackberry and Apple Jam

2 lbs (1 kg) blackberries
2 lbs (1 kg) cooking apples
4 lbs (2 kg) sugar
¼ pt (150 ml) water

Peel, core and chop the apples and put in a preserving pan with the water. Cook gently until the apples are just becoming soft then add the blackberries. Simmer until all the fruit is soft, then stir in the warmed sugar. When it has dissolved, boil rapidly until setting point, pot and cover. If you want a seedless jam, cook both fruits separately and strain the blackberries before mixing the two pulps.

Raspberry Jam

3 lbs (1.5 kg) raspberries
3 lbs (1.5 kg) sugar

Put the raspberries into a preserving pan and heat gently, stirring occasionally, until they are boiling. Stir in the warmed sugar. When it has dissolved, boil rapidly until set. This should only take about 3–5 minutes. Pour into hot jars and cover. Yields about 5 lbs (2.5 kgs).

Loganberry Jam as Raspberry Jam

Rhubarb Ginger Jam

3 lbs (1.5 kg) rhubarb
3 lbs (1.5 kg) sugar
Grated rind and juice of 3 lemons
4 oz (125 gm) chopped crystallized ginger

Wash and trim the rhubarb and cut into 1 inch pieces. Put with 1 lb (500 gm) sugar in a covered casserole and cook in a slow oven for 20 minutes, until the fruit is soft but still whole. Pour the rhubarb and juice into a preserving pan with the rest of the sugar, rind and juice of the lemons and the crystallized ginger. Heat gently, stirring until the sugar has dissolved, then boil rapidly for about 30 minutes or until the jam has reached setting point. Pour into hot jars and cover. Yields about 4 lbs (2 kg).

Chopped mixed candied peel can be used instead of the crystallized ginger, or a mixture of both.

Apple Ginger Jam

3 lbs (1.5 kg) apples
1 pt (600 ml) water
3 lbs (1.5 kg) sugar
1 oz (25 gm) root ginger
Grated rind and juice of 2 lemons
4 oz (125 gm) crystallized ginger

Peel, core and slice the apples. Bruise the root ginger and tie it with the peel and cores in a muslin bag. Put the apples, water, muslin bag, and rind and juice of the lemons in a preserving pan. Simmer until tender, remove the muslin bag and add the chopped crystallized ginger and sugar. Stir over a low heat until the sugar has dissolved, then boil rapidly until setting point is reached. Pour into hot jars and cover. Yields about 5 lbs (2.5 kg).

Marrow and Ginger Jam

3 lbs (1.5 kg) marrow
3 lbs (1.5 kg) sugar
2 lemons
1 oz (25 g) root ginger

Peel the marrow, remove the seeds and cut into inch cubes. Put in layers with the sugar in a large bowl and leave overnight. Peel the rind of the lemons, excluding the pith, and tie in a muslin bag with the bruised root ginger. Put the marrow and juices in a preserving pan with the muslin bag and bring slowly to the boil and add the lemon juice and sugar. When the sugar has dissolved, continue simmering until the marrow looks clear and the syrup is thick. Stir occasionally while simmering to prevent the jam sticking to the bottom of the pan. Remove the muslin bag, pour into hot jars and cover. Yields about 5 lbs (2.5 kg).

Pear and Peach Jam

1 lb (500 gm) pears
1 lb (500 gm) peaches
2 lbs (1 kg) sugar
Grated rind and juice 2 lemons
Water

Peel and core the pears and skin and stone the peaches. Chop both fruits into even sized pieces. Put into a preserving pan with just enough water to cover the bottom of the pan, and simmer gently until they are tender. Add the sugar, grated rind and juice of the lemons and stir over a low heat until the sugar has dissolved. Boil rapidly, stirring occasionally until setting point is reached. This should take about 20 minutes. Pour into hot jars and cover. Yields about 3 lbs (1.5

Plum Jam (using commercial pectin)

5 lbs (2.5 kg) plums
½ pt (300 ml) water
6½ lbs (3.25 kg) sugar
½ bottle commercial pectin

Wash the plums and chop into pieces. Put the fruit and water into a preserving pan, and if wanted, some of the stones may be cracked and the kernels added to the pan. Bring to the boil and simmer until tender. Add the warmed sugar, stir till dissolved, then boil rapidly for 4 minutes. Remove from the heat and stir in the commercial pectin. Allow to cool slightly to distribute the fruit evenly. Pour into hot jars, cover and label. Yields about 11 lbs.

Strawberry Jam (Using commercial pectin)

4 lbs (2 kg) strawberries
4 lbs (2 kg) sugar
½ pt (300 ml) commercial pectin

Hull the strawberries and put in a pan with the sugar. Heat gently, stirring until the sugar has dissolved. Add the pectin and boil rapidly until setting point. Pot and cover. Yields about 5 lbs (2.5 kg).

Black Cherry Jam (Using commercial pectin)

2½ lbs (1.25 kg) black cherries
2 lemons
¼ pt (150 ml) water
3 lbs (1.5 kg) sugar
1 bottle commercial pectin

Wash and stone the cherries, squeeze the lemons. Put the cherries, lemon juice and water in a covered pan and simmer gently for 15 minutes. Remove the lid, add the warmed sugar, and stir until dissolved. Boil rapidly for 4 minutes. Remove from the stove, stir in the pectin, and cool for 10–15 minutes before potting. Cover and label. Yields about 5 lbs (2.5 kg).

Sloe and Apple Jelly

4 lbs (2 kgs) cooking apples
2 lbs (1 kg) sloes
Juice and peel of 1 lemon
Sugar

Chop the washed apples, including the skins, and simmer in a pan with just enough water to cover, until they are soft and pulpy. Prick the washed sloes with a fork, and put in a separate pan, with enough water to cover, and the peel and juice of the lemon. Simmer until pulpy. Strain the two fruit pulps in a jelly bag and measure the juice. To each pint of juice, add 1 lb sugar, (750 gm to 1 litre). Bring to the boil stirring until dissolved. Boil, to setting point.

Bramble Jelly

4 lbs (2 kg) blackberries
Juice of 2 lemons, or 2 tsp citric acid
¾ pt (450 ml) water
Sugar

Simmer the washed and drained blackberries with the water and lemon juice until tender, about 30 minutes. Pour into a jelly bag, and strain overnight. Measure the juice. Bring the juice to the boil, and then add 1 lb warmed sugar to each pint. (750 gm to 1 litre). Stir until the sugar has dissolved, then boil rapidly until setting point. This should take about 10 minutes. Pour into hot jars and cover.

Crab Apple Jelly

6 lbs (3 kg) crab apples
Juice of 1 lemon
Sugar

Remove the stalks from the apples and wash well. Cut into pieces and put in a pan with the lemon juice and water to cover. Simmer until they are really tender, occasionally stirring and crushing the fruit. Strain in a jelly bag, then measure the juice. Bring the juice to the boil before adding 1 lb warmed sugar to each pint, (750 gm to 1 litre) Stir until the sugar has dissolved then boil rapidly until setting point.

Quince Jelly

4 lbs (2 kg) quinces
Water
Sugar
Juice of 2 lemons or 2 tsps citric acid

Wash the quinces. Cut into small pieces and put into a pan with enough cold water to barely cover. Simmer until quite tender, then strain overnight in a jelly bag. Next day measure the juice and to each pint allow 1 lb sugar (750 gm to 1 litre). Put the juice, sugar and lemon juice into a pan, bring slowly to the boil stirring, until the sugar has dissolved, then boil rapidly until setting point is reached.

Rose Petal Jelly

2 lbs (1 kg) cooking apples
1 oz (25 gm) dark red rose petals
1 pt (600 ml) water
Juice of half a lemon
Sugar

Cook the roughly chopped apples with the water and lemon juice until they are soft and pulpy. Strain through a jelly bag. Rinse the rose petals carefully and remove the pale bases, then dry thoroughly in a towel or on absorbent kitchen paper. Pound the petals with 2 tsps of sugar until well broken up, put in a pan with ¼ pt (150 ml) of water and simmer, covered, for about 15 minutes. Strain in a fine sieve. Measure the two batches of juices together, and to each pint, add 1 lb sugar (750 gm to 1 litre). Bring to the boil stirring well until the sugar has dissolved, then boil rapidly until setting point.

Redcurrant Jelly

4 lbs (2 kg) redcurrants
Sugar

Simmer the fruit very gently until the juice has run well. Strain overnight in a jelly bag. Measure the juice and bring it to the boil before adding 1 lb of warmed sugar for each pint (750 gm to 1 litre). Stir well, and as soon as the sugar has melted, pour into hot jars and cover.

Muscat Jelly

3 lbs (1.5 kg) gooseberries
1 pt (600 ml) water
Sugar
6 elderflower heads

Wash the gooseberries, there is no need to top and tail them, and put in a pan with the water. Simmer until they are soft and pulpy. Pour into a jelly bag and leave to drain overnight. Measure the juice, and to each 1 pt (600 ml) allow 1 lb (500 gm) sugar. Bring the juice and sugar slowly to the boil stirring till dissolved, then add the elderflower heads tied in a muslin bag. Continue boiling until setting point, remove the muslin bag, pot and cover.

Rowan Jelly

3 lbs (1.5 kg) ripe, red rowanberries
Sugar
Water
Juice of 1 lemon

Remove the stalks from the rowanberries and wash them. Put in a preserving pan with enough water to cover, and simmer till soft. Strain overnight in a jelly bag. Measure the juice and to each pint (600 ml) add 1 lb (500 gm) sugar. Put the juice, sugar and lemon juice into a pan, heat gently stirring until the sugar has dissolved, then boil rapidly until setting point. This should take about 30 minutes. Pour into hot jars and seal. Rowan jelly is excellent with game or cold meats, instead of redcurrant jelly.

Herb Jellies

3 lbs (1.5 kg) cooking apples
1 pt (600 ml) white wine vinegar
2 pts (1.2 litres) water
Sugar
½ cup chosen chopped herb to each 1 lb (500 gm) of apple jelly
few drops green food colouring (optional)

Wash and chop the apples, including the skins, and put in a preserving pan with the vinegar and water. Bring to the boil and simmer until the apples are very soft. Strain through a jelly bag overnight. Measure the juice and add 1 lb (500 gm) sugar to each 1 pt (600 ml). Heat gently, stirring till dissolved, then boil rapidly until setting point. Stir in the chopped herb and the colouring, remove any scum and allow to cool slightly before stirring again and potting. Cover and label.

Serve mint or rosemary jelly with lamb, sage jelly with pork, thyme jelly with poultry and parsley jelly with ham.

Seville Orange Marmalade

There are various methods for making this basic Seville orange marmalade, and after trying most of them, we have found that this is the most successful and economical recipe.

12 Seville oranges
2 sweet oranges
2 lemons
Water
Sugar, preserving or granulated

Wash all the fruit well and cut in halves. Squeeze out all the juice and put in a large bowl. Put the pips in a separate bowl, cover with boiling water and put a plate over. Slice all the peel very finely and put in the bowl with the juice. Measure the mixture and to each pint put 3 pts (1.8 litres) cold water. Cover and leave until the next day. Next day, boil the pips with their liquid for 5 minutes, then strain and put the strained liquid with the peel mixture. Put all into a preserving pan and boil until the peel is transparent and soft, and the liquid is reduced by at least a third, about 2½–3 hours slow boiling. Pour back into a large bowl and leave another night. Next day, measure the mixture back into the pan, and to every pint put 1 lb sugar (750 gm to 1 litre). Heat gently until the sugar has dissolved, then bring to the boil, and boil rapidly until setting point is reached, about 30–40 minutes. Leave to stand for 10–15 minutes until the peel is evenly distributed. Pour into hot jars and cover.

If you like a dark old English marmalade, add 2 tablespoons of black treacle with the sugar, or substitute all the white sugar for soft dark brown sugar. Yields about 12 lbs (6 kgs).

Three Fruit Marmalade

Use medium sized fruit
1 Grapefruit
2 Lemons
1 Sweet orange
2½ pts (1.5 litres) water
2½ lbs (1.25 kg) sugar

Wash the fruit well and cut in half. Squeeze out the juice and tie the pips in a muslin bag. Shred the peel finely and put in a preserving pan with the juice, water and muslin bag. Cover and leave to soak overnight. The next day bring to the boil and simmer until the peel is soft, about 1½ hours. Remove the muslin bag, squeezing gently to extract the pectin. Stir in the sugar and cook over a gentle heat until dissolved, then boil rapidly until setting point is reached, about 15–20 minutes. Leave to stand for 10–15 minutes until the peel is evenly distributed. Pour into hot jars and cover. Yields about 4 lbs (2 kg).

Alternative One Day Method

Wash the fruit well and put in a covered pan with the water. Simmer slowly until the skin is easily pierced with a wooden spoon handle or skewer, about 1½ hours. Remove the fruit from the liquid, allow to cool, then shred finely using a knife and fork, and reserving the pips. Put the pips into the liquid and boil for 10 minutes to extract the pectin. Remove the pips and put the cut fruit pulp, sugar and liquid into a preserving pan. Cook gently stirring until the sugar has dissolved, then bring to the boil and boil rapidly until setting point is reached, about 15–20 minutes. Leave to stand for about 10 minutes until the peel is evenly distributed, then pot, cover and label.

Apricot Marmalade

1 lb (500 gm) Seville or Sweet oranges
1 lb (500 gm) lemons
1 lb (500 gm) dried apricots
6 pts (3.5 litres) water
6 lbs (3 kg) sugar

Wash the fruit, cut the oranges and lemons in

half, squeeze out the juice and tie the pips in a muslin bag. Shred the orange and lemon peel and chop the apricots. Put all the fruit, juice, muslin bag and water into a preserving pan and bring to the boil. Simmer until the fruit is soft, about 1½–2 hours. Remove the muslin bag, squeezing the juice back into the pan to extract the pectin. Add the warmed sugar, stir till dissolved, then boil rapidly until setting point. Allow to stand for 10 minutes before potting. Yields about 10 lbs (5 kgs).

Grapefruit Marmalade

2 lbs (1 kg) grapefruit
1 lb (500 gm) lemons
6 pts (3.5 litres) water
6 lbs (3 kg) sugar

Wash the fruit well. Pare off the rind of the grapefruit and lemons, and cut into fine shreds. Cut the pith from the fruit, and tie with the pips in a muslin bag. Chop the flesh and put in a preserving pan with the shredded peel, muslin bag and the water. Bring to the boil and simmer until really tender, about 1–1½ hours. Remove the muslin bag, squeezing as much juice as possible back into the pan, to extract the pectin. Add the warmed sugar and stir over a low heat until dissolved. Boil rapidly until setting point. Remove the scum and allow to cool for 10–15 minutes to distribute the peel evenly. Pour into hot jars, cover and label. Yields about 10 lbs.

Tangerine Marmalade

2 lbs (1 kg) tangerines
1 lb (500 gm) lemons
6 pts (3.5 litres) water
6 lbs sugar

Wash the fruit, cut in half and squeeze out the juice. Tie the pips in a muslin bag. Finely shred the tangerine and lemon peels, including the pith, and put in a preserving pan with the juice, muslin bag and water. Bring to the boil, and simmer until tender, 1–1½ hours. Remove the muslin bag, squeezing the juice back into the pan. Add the warmed sugar, stir until dissolved, then boil rapidly until setting point. Remove any scum, and allow to cool slightly before pouring into hot jars. Cover and label. Yields about 10 lbs (5 kgs).

Jelly Marmalade

2 lbs (1 kg) Seville or Sweet oranges
1 lb (500 gm) lemons
Juice of 3 extra lemons or 2 tsps citric acid
6 pts (3.5 litres) water
Sugar

Wash the fruit and thinly peel the rind of the oranges and lemons, excluding the pith. Finely shred the rind and tie in a muslin bag. Cut up the remainder of the fruit. Put the muslin bag, fruit, including the pips and pith, lemon juice and water into a pan and bring to the boil. Simmer until very soft, about 1½ hours. Take out the muslin bag, reserving the peel for next day. Pour the rest of the fruit pulp into a jelly bag and leave to drip overnight. Measure the juice and to each pint add 1 lb sugar (750 gm

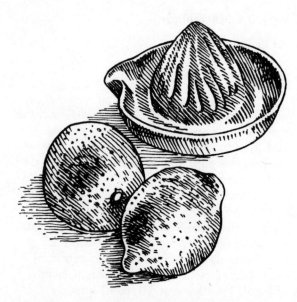

to 1 litre). Stir over a gentle heat until the sugar has dissolved, add the shredded peel and boil rapidly until setting point. Allow to cool before pouring into warmed jars, cover and label. Yields about 4½ lbs (2.25 kg).

Ginger Marmalade

2 lbs (1 kg) Seville or Sweet oranges
1 lb (500 gm) lemons
6 pts (3.5 litres) water
6 lbs (3 kg) sugar
1 oz (25 gm) root ginger
8 ozs (250 gm) preserved ginger

Wash the fruit and cut in half. Squeeze out the juice and finely shred the peel. Bruise or chop the root ginger and tie with the pips in a muslin bag. Put the peel, juice, muslin bag and water into a pan, bring to the boil, and simmer until the peel is very soft, about 1½ hours. Remove the muslin bag, add the warmed sugar and the finely chopped preserved ginger, then stir until the sugar has dissolved. Boil rapidly until setting point. Allow to stand for 10 minutes before potting. Yields about 10 lbs (5 kg).

Lemon Marmalade

2 lbs (1 kg) lemons
5 pts (3 litres) water
5 lbs (2.5 kg) sugar

Wash the lemons and put in a covered pan with the water. Simmer gently until the skins of the lemons can easily be pierced with a wooden spoon handle or skewer, about 1½–2 hours. Remove the lemons and allow to cool before shredding finely. Return the pips to the liquid and boil for 10 minutes. Remove the pips and put the cut lemon pulp back into the liquid. Bring to the boil, then add the warmed sugar. Stir until dissolved, then boil rapidly until setting point, about 15–20 minutes. Allow to stand for 10 minutes before pouring into hot jars. Cover and label. Yields about 7lbs (3.5 kg).

Carrot Marmalade

3 lbs (1.5 kg) carrots
Sugar
Lemons
Water

Cook the scraped and diced carrots in lightly salted water to cover, until they are soft. Rub through a sieve, measure, and return to a clean pan. Add 1 lb sugar and the grated rind

and juice of 2 lemons for each 1 lb of pulp
(750 gm to 1 litre). Stir over a gentle heat
until the sugar has dissolved, then cook until
thick. If you have it, 2 tblsp brandy may be
stirred in at this point. Pot, cover and label.
This marmalade improves with keeping.

Tomato Marmalade

3 lbs (1.5 kg) firm, ripe tomatoes
3 lbs (1.5 kg) sugar
3 lemons

Skin and slice the tomatoes. Grate the rind of
1 lemon and squeeze the juice of all three.
Simmer the tomatoes with the rind and juice
until they are soft, about 1 hour. Add the
warmed sugar, stir until dissolved, then boil
rapidly until set. Pour into warmed jars and
cover when cold.

Curds, Cheeses and Butters

Curds Cheeses and Butters

These are not so well known as jams and jellies—except perhaps for lemon curd—but they are useful to have in the storecupboard for a change, and to use up any surplus fruit you may have after making enough jam.

They are not terribly economic, because the yield from the fruit is much smaller than it would be for jam. On the other hand, in the case of cheeses and butters there is less preparation. The fruit is sieved after cooking, so there is no need to peel, stone, or even core it beforehand. Because of this they are a particularly good way of utilizing fruit like damsons and blackberries whose pips and stones can otherwise be an endless source of irritation.

The equipment needed is much the same as for jam, the only addition being a fine mesh nylon or plastic sieve. Do not use a metal one.

Curds

These take the form of a rich fruit puree cooked with the addition of butter and eggs. They are made in a double saucepan, or in a basin over a pan of boiling water, as the mixture must not be boiled to avoid curdling the eggs.

Because butter and eggs are added, the storage life is short. So they must be checked regularly for signs of deterioration. Carefully stored they will keep for one month. In a refrigerator, two or even three times longer.

Use them as you would jam. Spread on bread and butter, or as a tasty filling for tarts and sponges.

Cheeses

With their thick and firm consistency they make an unusual and delicious accompaniment for cold meats, poultry and game. Or you can serve them with bread instead of the cheese course. Which, back in Victorian days, is how they got their name.

Being a mixture of equal quantities of fruit pulp and sugar they have a long storage life. About 2 years. In fact the flavour improves greatly if they are kept for at least two months before you even think of using them.

Store in oiled jars, pots, or moulds, covered as for jam.

Serve by turning out whole from the jar and

cutting into slices at the table.

Cheeses should be stirred constantly while cooking, as the mixture tends to stick to the bottom of the pan. They are ready to pot when a clean line gradually falls back after a wooden spoon is drawn across the bottom of the pan.

Butters

Butters are not as thick as cheeses, and should be the consistency of cream so that they will spread nicely. Less sugar is used in proportion to the fruit pulp than for cheeses. So butters will only keep for 3 or 4 months. Once the jars are opened, the contents should be used within a few days. They are potted and covered in the same way as jam.

Lemon Curd

2 large lemons
6 oz (175 gm) caster sugar
3 large fresh eggs
3 oz (80 gm) butter

Finely grate the rinds of the lemons and squeeze out all the juice. Put the rind and sugar into a basin. Thoroughly whisk the eggs with the lemon juice and add to the basin. Next add the butter cut into small pieces. Fit the basin over a pan of simmering water and stir continuously until the curd thickens, this should take about 20 minutes. Pour into warmed jars and cover when cold.

Mock Lemon Curd

Small marrow
Lemons
Sugar
Butter
Eggs

Skin, de-seed and cut up the marrow. Put into a saucepan with a very little water to just cover the bottom of the pan. Simmer until soft. Weigh the pulp and to each 1 lb (500 gm) add the grated rind and juice of 2 lemons, 1 lb (500 gm) sugar, 4 oz (125 gm) butter and 2 large eggs. Put all the ingredients into a bowl and fit the bowl over a pan of simmering water. Cook gently stirring until smooth and thick. Pot and cover when cold.

Orange Curd

Use the recipe for Lemon curd, replacing the lemons by oranges, but adding the juice of ½ a lemon.

Blackberry Curd

1 lb blackberries
8 oz (250 gm) cooking apples
1 lb (500 gm) sugar
12 oz (350 gm) butter
4 eggs
1 lemon

Peel, core and chop the apples, and put with the blackberries in a pan. Cook until soft. Rub the fruit through a sieve and put the puree in a basin with the grated rind and juice of the lemon, the butter and sugar. Put over a pan of simmering water, and heat gently stirring until the sugar has dissolved. Add the lightly beaten eggs and continue cooking and stirring until the mixture thickens. Pour into prepared jars and cover.

Spiced Apple Curd

1 lb (500 gm) cooking apples
1 lemon
12 oz (350 gm) caster sugar
4 oz (125 gm) butter
4 eggs
1 tsp ground ginger
1 tsp ground cinnamon

Peel, core and slice the apples. Grate the rind and squeeze the juice of the lemon. Put the apples, rind and juice in a pan and simmer gently until the apples are soft and pulpy. Put through a sieve, or beat with a wooden spoon until really smooth. Lightly beat the eggs. Cut

up the butter. Place the apple, eggs, butter, sugar and spices in a bowl and put over a pan of simmering water. Stir well to dissolve the sugar and melt the butter. Continue cooking and stirring until the mixture is thick enough to coat the back of a wooden spoon. Pour into warm jars and cover.

Apricot Curd

8 oz (250 gm) fresh apricots
8 oz (250 gm) caster sugar
2 oz (50 gm) butter
2 large eggs
1 lemon

Put the washed apricots into a pan with just enough water to cover the bottom of the pan. Simmer until soft then sieve. Put the pulp into a bowl with the sugar, butter, juice and grated rind of the lemon. Put the bowl over a pan of simmering water and when the sugar has dissolved, add the beaten eggs. Continue stirring until the mixture thickens. Pot and cover.

Blackberry Cheese

1 lb (500 gm) cooking apples
2 lbs (1 kg) blackberries
¼ pt (150 ml) water
Sugar

Simmer the roughly chopped apples and the blackberries in the water until they are soft. Put through a sieve and weigh the pulp. To each 1 lb pulp add 1 lb sugar. (750 gm to 1 litre). Put all in a pan and heat, stirring until the sugar has dissolved. Boil gently until thick. Pour into warmed jars and cover.

Damson Cheese

2 lbs (1 kg) damsons
¼ pt (150 ml) water
Sugar

Simmer the cleaned fruit with the water until very soft and pulpy. Sieve and weigh the pulp. To each 1 lb of pulp add 1 lb of sugar (750 gm to 1 litre). Stir over heat until the sugar dissolves, then boil gently, stirring constantly until thick. This will take about 1 hour. Pot into small jars and cover.

Apple Cheese recipe as for Damson Cheese.

Quince Cheese recipe as for Damson Cheese.

Apple Butter

3 lbs (1.5 kg) cooking apples or crab apples
2 pts (1.2 litres) water or 1 pt (600 ml) water and 1 pt (600 ml) cider
Sugar
½ tsp ground cloves
½ tsp ground ginger

Wash and chop the apples, including the peel, and put in a large covered pan with the water, or water and cider. Simmer gently until very soft and pulpy, then rub through a fine sieve. Weigh the pulp, and to each 1 lb (500 gm) allow 12 oz (375 gm) sugar. Return the pulp to the pan with the sugar, cloves and ginger and stir over a gentle heat until the sugar has dissolved. Simmer until creamy in texture. Pot and cover.

Apple and Damson Butter

3 lbs (1.5 kg) cooking apples
1 lb (500 gm) damsons
Sugar

Wash and chop the apples, including the peel, wash and remove the stalks from the damsons. Put all the fruit in a large covered pan with just enough water to cover the base. Simmer gently until very tender. Rub the fruit through a fine sieve and weigh the pulp. Add 12 oz (375 gm) sugar for each 1 lb (500 gm) pulp. Heat the fruit and sugar together stirring until the sugar has dissolved. Simmer gently, stirring occasionally until the fruit is thick and creamy. Pot and cover.

Plum Butter

2 lbs (1 kg) plums
Sugar

Stalk and wash the plums and simmer gently with a very little water until soft. Rub through a fine sieve and weigh the pulp. To each 1 lb (500 gm) pulp allow 12 oz (375 gm) sugar. Heat the pulp and sugar together stirring, and when the sugar is dissolved, continue simmering until the butter is thick. Pot and cover.

Bramble Butter

2 lbs (1 kg) cooking apples or crab apples
2 lbs (1 kg) blackberries
Grated rind and juice of 1 large lemon
Sugar

Wash and roughly chop the apples, including the skins, and simmer with the blackberries, lemon rind and juice, in a covered saucepan until soft and pulpy. Rub through a sieve and weigh the pulp. To each 1 lb (500 gm) add 12 oz (375 gm) sugar. Bring slowly to the boil, stirring until the sugar has dissolved. Continue simmering and when thick and creamy pour into prepared jars and cover.

Quince Butter

3 lbs (1.5 kg) Quinces
Water
Sugar
1 level tsp citric acid

Wash and peel the quinces and chop into pieces. Put into a pan with the citric acid and enough water to nearly cover. Simmer gently until the fruit is very soft. Press through a sieve and weigh the pulp. Add 8 ozs (250 gm) sugar to each 1 lb (500 gm) pulp. Heat the fruit and sugar together, stirring until the sugar has dissolved. Continue boiling for about 1 hour until thick. Pot and cover.

Tomato Butter

2 lbs (1 kg) ripe tomatoes
Juice of 2 lemons
Sugar

Chop the tomatoes and simmer with the lemon juice until soft. Put through a fine sieve and measure the pulp. To each 1 lb (500 gm) pulp add 8 oz (250 gm) sugar. Cook gently stirring till dissolved, then simmer until thick. Pot and cover.

Mincemeat, Candied and Crystallized Fruit

Mincemeat, Candied & Crystallized Fruit—Crystallized Flowers

Mincemeat

Mincemeat is the delicious mixture of dried and fresh fruits, spices, suet, sugar and alcohol that most of us eat only once a year in our Christmas pies. Of course it tastes equally delicious at other times of the year, but the main drawback to this is that it is not cheap to make. However, this can be overcome by mixing it with other fruits such as apples or apricots for pies and crumbles. It also combines well with walnuts.

Mincemeat was originally a mixture of minced beef, spices and fruits, but it would not have kept anywhere near as long as our present day brew which will last from one year to the next.

Store mincemeat as you would jam.

Mincemeat

8 oz (250 gm) stoned raisins
6 oz (175 gm) sultanas
6 oz (175 gm) currants
4 oz (125 gm) chopped mixed peel
2 oz (50 gm) blanched almonds
6 oz (175 gm) beef suet
8 oz (250 gm) cooking apples
1 small orange
1 small lemon
6 oz (175 gm) dark soft brown sugar
¼ level tsp salt
½ level tsp nutmeg
½ level tsp cinnamon
½ level tsp mixed spice
4 tblsp brandy

Put the raisins and some of the sultanas through a mincer. Finely chop the almonds and chop or grate the suet. Wash, core and peel the apples, and grate or dice into small pieces. Put all the fruits, almonds and suet in a large bowl. Grate the rinds of the orange and lemon, squeeze out the juices, and add to the

need it for a truly professional finish. But you don't have to bother to buy it anymore, because it is very easily made at home for next to nothing. Just think of all that orange peel you throw away. Well, with the addition of sugar, and a little effort on your part, it can be transformed very easily into candied peel. The process is quite a long drawn out one, but don't let that put you off. It may well take a few days to complete, but there will be very little for you to do each day.

Glacé cherries and angelica are expensive to buy, so if supplies of fresh cherries and angelica* are available it is well worth making them.

Marrons Glacé (candied chestnuts) and crystallized fruits are probably only known as a special treat at Christmas, or perhaps you have never even tasted them they are so expensive to buy. Particularly crystallized fruits. But they cost little to make, and can easily be added to your regular treat list.

Crystallized flowers are used as decorations for cakes and desserts. If you have to buy them, you probably hardly ever use them. But if you make your own, you can substitute them for other expensive cake decorations such as chocolate or nuts, so you will save money. There is no heating involved in making them.

Select flowers for crystallizing with care, consult your field guide to make sure they are

mixture in the bowl. Finally, add the salt, spices and brandy. Mix well, cover and leave overnight. Next day, mix well again. Pack into jars, cover and label, and store in a cool, dry cupboard. Makes approximately 4 lbs (2 kgs).

Candied Fruit, Crystallized Fruit and Flowers

Most housewives who are at all keen on cooking use candied peel as an embellishment that adds that final touch to their baking masterpieces. And true enough, you really do

---

*   Angelica is the candied stem of the plant of the same name. One species grows in the wild, but it is from the cultivated variety that the best candied angelica can be made.

not poisonous, and that you are not breaking the law by gathering a protected species. As a general rule it will be best if you use only suitable cultivated varieties.

Method

The method for candying or crystallizing is basically the same. The fruits are tenderized if necessary, and left in boiled syrup overnight. This process is repeated several times adding more sugar to the syrup each day and re-boiling it. The fruit are left overnight soaking in the syrup. The object is to create layer upon layer of crystallized sugar all over the fruit to preserve them.

Candied Peel

3 oranges
3 lemons
½ oz (12.5 gm) bicarbonate of soda
1½ lbs (750 gm) granulated sugar

Wash the fruit well and cut the oranges in half, crosswise, and the lemons, lengthwise. Take out all the pulp. Put the peels in a large bowl. Dissolve the bicarbonate of soda in ¼ pt (150 ml) of hot water and pour over the peel. Top up the bowl with more boiling water to completely cover the peel. Stand aside for 25 minutes, then drain and rinse the peel. Put in a saucepan, cover with cold water, bring to the boil and simmer until tender. Make a syrup in a separate pan with 1 lb (500 gm) of the sugar and ¾ pt (450 ml) of water. Drain the peel, return to the bowl and pour over the syrup. Leave to stand for 2 days. Strain the syrup back into a pan, add the rest of the

sugar, and bring to the boil over a gentle heat. Put in the peel and simmer until it is transparent. Lift the peel out with a draining spoon, put it on trays to dry out in a low oven. Boil up the syrup again for 30 minutes, remove from the heat. Dip the peel in the syrup, lift out and dry again in the oven. Simmer the remaining syrup until it is thick and cloudy, pour a little into each dried peel cup and leave to dry. Store in airtight containers.

Marrons Glacé

1 lb (500 gm) chestnuts
1 lb (500 gm) granulated sugar
½ pt (300 ml) water
1 vanilla pod or ½ tsp vanilla essence

Remove the outer skins of the chestnuts. Put them in a pan of water to cover, bring to the boil and simmer for 20 minutes. Peel while they are warm. Make a syrup with the sugar and water. Stir until the sugar has dissolved, bring to the boil and simmer for 5 minutes. Add the chestnuts and the vanilla, and boil rapidly for 10 minutes. Leave for 24 hours. Next day, re-boil the syrup and nuts, and simmer until they are thoroughly coated. Take out the nuts with a draining spoon and dry on a wire rack. Store in an airtight container, or wrap individually in foil.

Candied Angelica

Choose young stalks of the angelica plant. Cut them into even lengths and boil in water until tender. Take them out of the water and peel off the outer skin. Return to the pan and simmer gently until the stalks turn green. Drain. Leave them to dry and weigh. For each 1 lb (500 gm) of angelica, allow 1 lb (500 gm) granulated sugar. Put the angelica in a shallow bowl and sprinkle on the sugar. Cover and leave to stand for 2 days. Put all the contents of the bowl into a pan, bring to the boil and simmer for about 10 minutes. Remove the angelica with a draining spoon, add another 2 ozs (50 gm) sugar to the syrup, stir till dissolved then bring to the boil. Put the angelica back in the pan and simmer for 10 minutes. Drain the angelica and put on trays in a cool oven to dry. Store in an airtight container, and use for decorating cakes and desserts.

Glacé Cherries

Carefully remove the stones from some red

cherries, taking care to keep the fruits as whole as possible. Simmer them very gently until just tender, drain and dry thoroughly. Brush them all over with gum arabic, sprinkle with a very little granulated sugar and leave to dry. Store in an airtight jar and use for decorating cakes and desserts.

Crystallized Flowers

The best flowers to use for crystallizing are violets, rose petals, primroses, lilac or fruit blossoms such as orange, apple, pear or plum. Be sure that whatever flower you use is not poisonous! Pick the flowers on a dry, sunny day. Mix 1 oz (25 gm) gum arabic with a little strong rosewater in a bowl. Leave to stand until the gum arabic has melted, this will take at least 1 day. Using a small brush, carefully paint each petal on both sides until they are thoroughly coated. Sprinkle each flower all over with a little caster sugar. Store in a container putting a sheet of greaseproof paper between each layer.

Crystallized Fruits

Fruits for crystallizing should be perfectly sound and not over-ripe. Carefully remove the stones from plums, damsons, greengages, cherries and apricots, keeping the fruits as whole as possible. Cut pineapple into chunks. Remove the peel and pith from oranges and lemons, and divide into their natural segments without breaking the inner skins. Leave a small stem on pears and grapes.

Make a syrup with 8 oz (250 gm) sugar to ½ pt (300 ml) water. To each 1 lb (500 gm) of fruit allow ½ pt (300 ml) syrup. While the syrup is warm, pour over the prepared fruits in a shallow dish, and leave to stand for 24 hours. Drain off the syrup into a pan, add another 2 oz (50 gm) sugar and bring to the boil stirring. Pour back over the fruit and leave for another day. Repeat this process for 3 more times over a period of 3 days, adding 2 oz (50 gm) sugar to the syrup each time it is re-boiled. Drain the syrup, and this time add 3 oz (80 gm) sugar to the syrup, and when it is boiling put in the fruit and simmer for 4 minutes. Repeat the boiling process with 3 oz (80 gm) sugar again the next day. Thoroughly drain the fruit and put on a wire cooling tray. Put the tray in a cool oven 100 C/200 F or Gas mark ¼ leaving the door open slightly. Take out when the coating is crisp and dry.

Store the fruits wrapped in waxed paper or foil, and put in airtight boxes.

An Alternative Method

Use slightly unripe fruit. Make a heavy syrup with 1 lb (500 gm) sugar to ½ pt (300 ml) water. Boil the syrup for 10 minutes, add the fruit and continue boiling until it is just tender and still holds its shape. Remove the pan from the heat. Leave the fruit in the syrup until it looks semi-transparent. Drain off the syrup and bring it back to the boil. Using a fine wooden skewer or coarse needle, immerse each fruit in the syrup. Lift out and drain on a wire cooling tray. Dry off the fruits and store as described in the first method.

Pickles and Chutneys

Pickles and Chutneys

Pickles

The most popular pickles are probably pickled onions, but virtually all vegetables and fruit can be pickled, as can some nuts and seeds, and eggs as well. Cultivated varieties are most popularly chosen for the process, but many types of wild produce can also be successfully pickled if you would like to try something out of the ordinary. Whether pickled by themselves or in combinations with others, the pickling process for all raw materials is typically the same. Relying mainly on the preservative ability of the acetic acid content of the vinegar.

Serving Ideas

Pickles can be used as an accompaniment to any cold meats, poultry or game, and they can also be served with cheese or mixed hors d'oeuvres. Fruit pickles being particularly delicious with game. Pickled nasturtium seeds are well paired with fish, and of course pickled eggs make an excellent snack with crisps or bread, or on their own.

Method

Vegetables for pickling are first prepared, sprinkled with coarse or block cooking salt, or put in a brine solution. This is left overnight to crisp the vegetables and extract the moisture, which is then drained off, or it would impair the preserving qualities of the vinegar. There is little or no cooking involved in pickling vegetables.

Fruits for pickling are usually cooked until they are just tender and still maintaining their shape.

Vinegar

Vinegar for pickling is better if it is spiced at least one month before using. But you won't have disasters if you use one of our quick methods for making spiced vinegar that we explain in Chapter Ten.

There are a variety of bottled vinegars which can be used, brown, malt, and white. Try white wine or cider vinegar as a change for pickling fruits. Any vinegar must be boiled at some stage or the pickles will not keep.

Filling the Jars

When the vegetables or fruits have been processed for pickling, they are packed carefully and tightly into prepared jars with the aid of a wooden spoon. Fill up to the necks. The vinegar is then poured in, covering the contents by at least ½″.

Covering the Jars

The jars should be covered with vinegar-proof, air-tight lids. Plastic ones are best as metal will taint the preserves if they come into contact with the vinegar. If the jars have no lids (or unsuitable ones) use 2 layers of greaseproof paper and a top layer of foil tied down securely with string.

Storing

Pickles will keep for at least 1 year if they are properly stored in a cool, dark place.

Chutneys

Chutneys differ from pickles in that the vegetables or fruits (or a combination of both) are cooked to a pulp instead of being left whole.

Chutneys are very versatile and can be eaten with any cold meats, served with cheese, or used in cooking. Some curry recipes include chutney, and they can also be used in making meat pies.

Method

After the vegetables or fruits have been pulped, vinegar, sugar, salt and spices are added as preservatives and flavourings. All the ingredients are cooked slowly together for 1½–3 hours until they have reached the consistency of jam and all the flavours are blended.

Although we give many recipes, don't be afraid to experiment with the spices used to suit your personal taste. Basically use more spices if you like a hot chutney.

Potting

Chutneys are potted while still hot into clean warmed jars and covered immediately. The covering rules are the same as for pickles.

Storing

Chutneys store very well, provided they are kept in a cool dark place. In fact some will keep for years if you can keep your hands off them! Most chutneys improve as they mature, so store for at least 3 months before using.

Equipment for making Pickles and Chutneys

You will need scales, and an aluminium or stainless steel preserving pan—or a large heavy bottomed saucepan. These should not be made of copper, iron or brass, as the vinegar used will corrode the metal and contaminate the food.

A large bowl for salting the vegetables overnight will also be necessary, as well as jars (wide necked ones for pickles), and airtight, vinegar-proof covers. And you will need some muslin for spice bags as well.

A mincer or shredder, and a funnel would also be useful for making chutneys, but they are not vital and you can manage quite well without them.

Pickled Shallots or Onions

Shallots or small pickling onions
Salt
Water
Spiced vinegar

Peel the shallots or onions with a stainless steel knife and put in a brine solution, using 2 oz (50 gm) of salt to 1 pt (600 ml) of water. Leave in the brine for at least 48 hours. Remove from the brine, rinse well in running cold water, then drain thoroughly. Pack tightly into jars and cover with cold spiced vinegar, making sure the vinegar comes at least ½″ above the onions. Pickled onions are better if allowed to mature for at least 3 months.

Pickled Eggs

Fresh eggs
Spiced vinegar, malt, distilled, red or white wine

Hard boil the eggs for 12 minutes, then place immediately under running cold water. When cold, carefully peel off the shells. Put in wide-necked jars. Do not pack tightly as there must be room for the vinegar to surround all of the eggs. Cover with cold spiced vinegar. Leave for 2 weeks before eating.

Pickled Walnuts

Young, green walnuts
Water
Salt
Spiced vinegar

Prick walnuts all over with a fork. Soak in a brine solution, using 8 oz (250 gm) salt to 1 pt (600 ml) water, for at least 3 days, preferably 9 days, changing the brine solution every 3 days. Drain well and spread on a tray and leave them exposed to the air or in the sun, until they are black. This can take 1–3 days. Pack into jars and cover with cold spiced vinegar. After 2 or 3 days it may be necessary to top up with more vinegar. Leave for at least 1 month before using.

Pickled Marrow

2 lbs (1 kg) marrow
½ lb (250 gm) cooking apples
½ lb (250 gm) onions
4 oz (125 gm) soft brown sugar
4 oz (125 gm) coarse salt
1½ tsp ground ginger
1 tsp curry powder
1 oz (25 gm) mustard powder
6 peppercorns
1 pt (600 ml) malt vinegar

Peel the marrow, remove the seeds and chop into small cubes. Sprinkle with the salt and leave overnight. Peel, core and chop the apples, peel and chop the onions. Simmer the apples and onions in a pan with the vinegar until softened, then add the ginger, curry powder, mustard, peppercorns and sugar.

Bring to the boil stirring and boil for 5 minutes. Add the rinsed and drained marrow cubes. Simmer until tender then pack into jars. Seal at once. The pickle can be used in 3–4 weeks.

Pickled Red Cabbage

2 lbs (1 kg) red cabbage
2 oz (50 gm) cooking salt
2 pts (1.2 litres) spiced vinegar

Using only the firm hearts of the cabbages, shred finely and put in layers with the salt in a bowl. Leave for 24 hours. Drain off the liquid and pack the cabbage into jars. Cover with cold spiced vinegar. Leave for 2 weeks before using.

Blackberry Pickle

2 lbs (1 kg) blackberries
1 lb (500 gm) granulated sugar
½ pt (300 ml) vinegar
1″ stick cinnamon
6 cloves
Small piece of whole ginger

Tie the spices in a muslin bag and put into a saucepan with the vinegar and simmer for 20 minutes, keeping the lid on the pan. Meanwhile, bring the blackberries and 4 ozs (125 gm) of the sugar gently to the boil in another pan. Add the rest of the sugar and stir gently until dissolved. Add the vinegar and spices to the blackberries and simmer very gently for 20–30 minutes, being careful not to break the fruit. Strain the blackberries and pack them into hot jars. Remove the muslin bag of spices. Quick boil the remaining vinegar and juices until it is a thick rich syrup and pour over the blackberries. If you have it, put a few pieces of horseradish on top of each jar and cover. This pickle is good with roast or grilled meat.

Pickled Damsons

2 lbs (1 kg) damsons
1½ lbs (750 gm) sugar
1 pt (600 ml) malt vinegar
1 large onion
1″ stick cinnamon
10 cloves

Wash and dry the damsons, removing any stalks, and prick each with a fork in several places. Put them with the sugar, in layers, in a large bowl. Pour over the vinegar, cover with a plate and leave for 24 hours. Next day, drain off the juice into a saucepan. Stick the cloves into the peeled onion and add it with the cinnamon stick to the juice and vinegar. Put the lid on the pan and simmer gently for an hour. Strain the liquid over the damsons, cover, and leave for a further 24 hours. Next day, boil the damsons and liquid rapidly for 10 minutes, taking care to keep the damsons whole. Pour into warm jars and cover. Yields about 3 lbs (1.5 kg). This sweet pickle is excellent with game, hare or cold meats.

Piccalilli

1 small cauliflower
1 small unpeeled cucumber
8 oz (250 gm) peeled and seeded marrow
8 oz (250 gm) peeled shallots
1 pt (600 ml) malt vinegar
1 oz (25 gm) salt
2 ozs (50 gm) sugar
1 level tblsp mustard powder
1tsp ground ginger
1 tsp turmeric
1½ oz (35 gm) flour

Divide the cauliflower into small florets and cut the marrow and cucumber into small cubes. Put all the vegetables into a large bowl, sprinkle with the salt and leave overnight.

Next day, drain the vegetables well. Blend the sugar, mustard powder, ginger, turmeric and flour with a little of the vinegar. Bring the remaining vinegar to the boil, pour over the paste stirring, then return to the pan. Bring to the boil stirring carefully and cook for 5 minutes. Add the drained vegetables and simmer gently for 10 minutes. Cool pickle slightly, then pour into warm jars. Cover when cold. Yields about 5 lbs (2.5 kg).

Pickled Mushrooms

1 lb (500 gm) button mushrooms
1 shallot or small onion
1 pt (600 ml) malt vinegar
Salt
½ tsp ground black pepper

Clean the mushrooms by wiping them with a damp cloth dipped in the salt. Put them into a pan over a low heat until the moisture starts running out of them. Peel and finely chop the onion and add to the pan with the remaining ingredients. Simmer gently until the mushrooms are tender. Spoon the mushrooms into a jar and pour over the strained hot vinegar and seal. Yields 1 lb (500 gm).

Mixed Pickles

1 cauliflower
1 cucumber
8 oz (250 gm) pickling onions
8 oz (250 gm) french beans
8 oz (250 gm) green tomatoes
3 pts (1.8 litres) water
8 oz (250 gm) salt
2½ pts (1.5 litres) spiced vinegar

Break the cauliflower into sprigs, cut the cucumber and tomatoes into cubes, peel the onions and top and tail the beans. Make a brine with the water and salt in a large bowl and put in the prepared vegetables. Leave for 24 hours. Drain, rinse well in cold water and drain again. Pack into jars and cover with cold spiced vinegar. Leave to stand for a little while then top up with more vinegar if necessary. Seal and label. Leave to mature for at least 1 month before using.

Pickled Beetroot

3 lbs (1.5 kg) uncooked beetroot
Spiced vinegar

Choose only beetroot with undamaged skin and wash carefully. Boil in lightly salted water until tender, about 1–1½ hours, depending on the size. Cool, rub off the skins and cut into slices. If the beetroot are very small they may be left whole. Pack into prepared jars and cover with cold spiced vinegar.

Bullace Pickle

3 lbs (1.5 kg) bullace (wild plums)
1 pt (600 ml) spiced vinegar
1½ lbs (750 gm) demerara sugar

Pack the bullace into preserving jars. Put in a moderate oven and cook until the skins begin to split. Boil the spiced vinegar and sugar together for 10 minutes, then pour it over the bullace. Cover when cold.

For a more spicey flavour, add a small piece of cinnamon stick and a few cloves when boiling the vinegar.

Chow-Chow

2 small or 1 large cucumber
1 medium cauliflower
1 hard cabbage, red or green
1 small head of celery
1 lb (500 gm) green tomatoes
1 lb (500 gm) peeled shallots or pickling onions
½ lb (250 gm) young french beans
2 ozs (50 gm) salt
2 pts (1.2 litres) malt vinegar
4 oz (125 gm) soft brown sugar
2 oz (50 gm) mustard powder
2 oz (50 gm) flour
1 dessertspoon turmeric
½ tsp cinnamon
½ tsp ground allspice
½ tsp ground cloves
pepper and salt
Horseradish

Shred the cabbage, break the cauliflower into small sprigs and chop the cucumber, celery, tomatoes, onions and beans into small pieces. Put all the vegetables into a large bowl, sprinkle with the salt and cover with water. Leave to soak overnight. Next day, drain, and rinse well in cold water. Turn into a large saucepan, add ¼ pt (150 ml) of the vinegar, top up with water and bring to the boil. Simmer for 15 minutes then drain off the liquid. Mix the sugar, mustard, flour, turmeric and spices to a smooth paste with some vinegar, heat the remainder. Pour the hot vinegar onto the paste, and mix until it is smooth. Pour back into the pan and bring to the boil slowly, stirring well until thick. Add the vegetables and a little grated horseradish and simmer for 10–15 minutes. Pour into hot jars, and cover when cold.

Pickled Nasturtium Seeds

A very good substitute for capers
Nasturtium seeds
1 pt (600 ml) vinegar
2 bay leaves
2 tsps salt
6 peppercorns

Gather the nasturtium seeds on a dry day. Wipe clean with a cloth, and dry in a very slow oven or on a tray in the sun. Put the bay leaves, salt and peppercorns into a pan with the vinegar and bring to the boil. Remove from the heat and allow to get cold before straining. Put the seeds into sterilized bottles, and cover with the vinegar. If there are not enough seeds to fill the bottle, more may be added as they are ready to be picked and dried. When the bottle is full, seal, and keep for at least 2 months before using.

Pickled Cucumbers

2 large or 4 small cucumbers
2 onions
1 green pepper
1 pt (600 ml) vinegar, malt, cider or white wine
8 oz (250 gm) sugar
2 oz (50 gm) salt
2 tblsp mustard seed
1 tsp turmeric

Cut the cucumbers into ¼″ slices, peel and slice the onions, remove the core and seeds

from the green peper and slice thinly. Put in layers in a bowl, sprinkle with the salt and leave overnight. Drain off the liquid, rinse well and drain again. Put the vinegar, sugar, mustard seed and turmeric into a pan, heat slowly stirring until the sugar has dissolved, then bring to the boil. Add the vegetables and simmer gently for 10 minutes. Spoon the pickle into prepared jars, top up with the vinegar and cover.

Beetroot Chutney

2 lbs (1 kg) uncooked beetroot
1 lb (500 gm) onions
1½ lbs (750 gm) cooking apples
1 lb (500 gm) seedless raisins or sultanas
3 tblsp ground ginger
2 lbs (1 kg) granulated sugar
2 pts (1.2 litres) malt vinegar

Peel and grate the beetroot, peel and finely

chop the onions. Peel, core and chop the apples. Put in a pan with the raisins, sugar, vinegar and ginger. Heat gently until the sugar has dissolved. Bring to the boil and simmer until thick, then pot and cover. Yields about 4 lbs (2 kg).

Pumpkin Chutney

2½ lbs (1.25 kg) pumpkin, prepared weight
1 lb (500 gm) red tomatoes
8 oz (250 gm) onions
4 oz (125 gm) sultanas
1½ lbs (750 gm) soft brown sugar
2½ tsp ground ginger
2 tsp ground black pepper
2 tsp ground allspice
2 garlic cloves
2½ tblsp salt
1 pt (600 ml) tarragon vinegar

Peel and slice the tomatoes and onions and cut the pumpkin flesh into small pieces. Put all in a pan with the sultanas, sugar, spices, crushed garlic, salt and vinegar. Stir over a gentle heat until the sugar has dissolved. Bring to the boil and simmer gently until soft and the chutney is the consistency of jam. Pot and cover. Yields about 4 lbs (2 kgs).

Uncooked Chutney

1½ lbs (750 gm) cooking apples
8 oz (250 gm) onions
1 lb (500 gm) raisins or sultanas
1½ lbs (750 gm) soft brown sugar
1 level tblsp salt
½ pt (300 ml) spiced malt vinegar

Peel and core the apples and put them through a mincer with the peeled and chopped onions and the raisins or sultanas. Put these ingredients in a large bowl with the sugar, salt and spiced vinegar. Cover and leave for 24 hours stirring occasionally until the sugar is dissolved. Pot and cover. Yields about 4½ lbs (2 kgs).

Although this chutney is uncooked, it will keep for at least a year.

Green Tomato Chutney

3 lbs (1.5 kg) green tomatoes
3 lbs (1.5 kg) cooking apples
3 lbs (1.5 kg) onions
1 lb (500 gm) sultanas
1 lb (500 gm) soft dark brown sugar
2½–3 pts (1.5–1.8 litres) malt vinegar
1 tblsp salt
2 tsp cayenne pepper
2½ tsp ginger (ground)
1 tsp mustard powder
2 tsp pickling spices

Finely chop the tomatoes and start simmering in a preserving pan with a pint of the vinegar. Meanwhile, finely chop the onions and add to the tomatoes with another pint of the vinegar. Finely chop the peeled and cored apples and add to the pan with the tomatoes and onions. Stir in the remaining vinegar, sultanas, salt, cayenne, ginger, mustard and the pickling spices tied in a muslin bag. When all the mixture is softened, add the sugar and stir well until dissolved. Bring to the boil and simmer for ½ hr–1 hr until the chutney is the consistency of jam. Pot in hot jars and cover. Yields about 9 lbs (4 kgs).

Chinese-style Mixed Fruit Chutney

1 large pineapple
2 lbs (1 kg) plums
2 lbs (1 kg) fresh apricots
2 lbs (1 kg) soft brown sugar
1 pt (600 ml) white wine vinegar

Peel the pineapple, discard the hard centre core. Skin and halve the plums and apricots and remove the stones. Cut all the fruit flesh into small pieces, and put into a pan with the sugar and about half the vinegar. Heat gently stirring until the sugar has dissolved. Simmer, stirring frequently and adding more vinegar if necessary, until the fruit is soft. Pot at once and cover. Yields about 6 lbs (3 kgs).

Hot Indian Chutney

2 lbs (1 kg) cooking apples
1 lb (500 gm) onions
1 lb (500 gm) stoned raisins
8 garlic cloves
4 pts (2.25 litres) malt vinegar

2 lbs (1 kg) soft dark brown sugar
2 oz (50 gm) salt
4 oz (125 gm) mustard powder
5 oz (150 gm) ground ginger
4 tsp cayenne pepper

Peel and chop the onions. Peel, core and slice the apples, and crush the garlic. Simmer the onions, apples, garlic, sugar and salt in the vinegar until soft. Rub through a sieve and put into a clean pan. Stir in the chopped raisins, mustard, ginger and cayenne pepper. Cover with a cloth and leave the mixture in a warm place or an airing cupboard overnight. Next day, stir, pot and cover. Yields 5 lbs (2.5 kgs).

Apple Chutney

6 lbs (3 kg) cooking apples
2 lbs (1 kg) onions
1 lb (500 gm) raisins or sultanas
2 lbs (1 kg) soft brown sugar
2½ pts (1.5 litres) vinegar
1½ oz (35 gm) salt
1½ oz (35 gm) ground ginger
1 tblsp ground cinnamon
1 tsp cayenne

Peel and chop the apples and onions, and simmer in 1½ pts (900 ml) of the vinegar until they are soft. Stir in the remaining vinegar, raisins, salt, ginger, cinnamon and cayenne, and simmer for a further 20 minutes. Finally add the sugar and stir until it has dissolved, then cook until thick, about ½ hr–1 hr. Pot into hot jars and cover. Yields about 8 lbs (4 kg).

Marrow Chutney

4 lbs (2 kg) prepared marrow
8 oz (250 gm) chopped onion
8 oz (250 gm) raisins or sultanas
1 lb (500 gm) sugar
2 pts (1.2 litres) vinegar
6 cloves
6 chillies
Small piece root ginger
1 oz (25 gm) mustard powder
1 oz (25 gm) turmeric
Salt

Cut the prepared marrow into small cubes, put into a large bowl and sprinkle with salt. Leave to stand overnight. Put the chopped onion in a pan with the vinegar, sugar and the cloves, chillies and root ginger tied in a muslin bag. Simmer for 15 minutes then add the drained marrow, mustard and turmeric. Continue cooking until the marrow is tender, remove the muslin bag, pot and cover.

Elderberry Chutney

2 lbs (1 kg) elderberries
8 oz (250 gm) chopped onion
4 oz (125 gm) raisins
8 oz (250 gm) sugar
1 pt (600 ml) vinegar
1 tsp salt
1 tsp ground ginger
1 tsp pickling spices
½ tsp cayenne
½ tsp mustard powder

Simmer the chopped onion in half the vinegar until soft. Strip the elderberries from the stalks, and add them to the onion together with the chopped raisins, salt, ginger, cayenne and mustard, and the pickling spices tied in muslin. Simmer until the mixture has softened. Add the sugar, stir well, and when dissolved, boil until the chutney is thick. Pot and cover when cold.

Rhubarb Chutney

4 lbs (2 kg) rhubarb
1 lb (500 gm) onions
1 lb (500 gm) soft brown sugar
1 pt (600 ml) vinegar
½ oz (12.5 gm) salt
½ oz (12.5 gm) ground ginger
½ oz (12.5 gm) curry powder

Simmer the prepared and chopped rhubarb and onions in a pan, with half the vinegar, salt, ginger and curry powder. Cook gently for about 1 hour. Add the rest of the vinegar and the sugar, stir and when dissolved, simmer for a further 45 minutes–hour. Pour into hot jars and seal. Yields about 4 lbs (2 kg).

Sauces and Vinegars

Sauces and Vinegars

Sauces are made with similar ingredients to chutneys, but when vegetables are used, they are sieved after cooking to make a pourable consistency. The fruit in sweet sauces—except blackberries—are left whole but are served with hot and cold meats in the same way as vegetable sauces are.

Homemade sauces are totally different from any that can be bought. Not only do they taste refreshingly wholesome and natural, but the range and variety of those that can be made opens up aspects of good eating that most people never knew even existed.

None are expensive to make, and many have the additional advantage that their main ingredient consists of the sort of produce that one is likely to have a glut of.

Equipment

A stainless steel or aluminium pan with a heavy base must be used, not brass, copper or iron, as these metals will react adversely with the vinegar. Sieves must be nylon or stainless steel.

You will also need scales, muslin, wooden spoons, a measuring jug, and bottles with screw tops or corks.

A funnel would also be useful, and you will need a grater if you are going to make horseradish sauce.

If you are sterilizing your full bottles you will also need a deep pan, a trivet or thick cloth, and paraffin wax if you are using corks.

Storing

If you want to keep your sauces for a long time, the bottles should really be sterilized before and after filling—as for syrups. If they are to be stored for a short period only, it is still necessary to sterilize the empty bottles and tops.

Store in a cool, dark cupboard.

Mint Sauce

8 oz (250 gm) mint leaves
Approx ½ pt (300 ml) malt vinegar

Wash, dry and finely chop the mint leaves. Pack into clean, dry jars, and pour in enough vinegar to cover the mint. Cover and label.

To make mint sauce as required: Take out enough mint as needed, add a little sugar, boiling water and vinegar.

Horseradish Sauce

1 or 2 large horseradish roots
Distilled malt vinegar

Wash, peel and grate the horseradish. Pack immediately into clean dry jars, then pour in enough vinegar to cover. Seal and label, and store in a cool dark place to preserve the colour.

To make horseradish sauce as required: Take out as much horseradish as needed, strain off the vinegar. Stir in a little cream, yogurt or soured cream and salt and pepper to taste.

Tomato Sauce

9 lbs (4.5 kg) red tomatoes
1 lb (500 gm) onions
5 garlic cloves
1½ oz (35 gm) salt
½ pt (300 ml) distilled malt vinegar
1 oz (25 gm) mustard powder
1 tsp mixed spice
1 tsp paprika
1 tsp cayenne
1½ lbs (750 gm) gran sugar

If you cannot get garlic cloves, use ¾ oz (15 gm) garlic salt and reduce the quantity of plain salt to ¾ oz (15 gm).

Peel and finely chop the onions, and coarsely chop the skinned tomatoes. Crush the garlic if used. Put into a large saucepan or a preserving pan and simmer for about 15 minutes. Add the vinegar, mustard powder, salt, mixed spice, paprika and cayenne. Stir well, bring to the boil and simmer for about 1 hour. Add the sugar and heat gently until dissolved, then simmer for 15 minutes. Pour into hot sterilized jars or bottles and seal. Yields about 7 lbs (3.5 kg).

Cumberland Sauce

4 oranges
2 lemons
1 dessertspoon finely chopped onion
1 lb (500 gm) redcurrant jelly
¼ pt (150 ml) port
1½ tblsp cornflour

Cut the peel from the oranges and lemons in large pieces, excluding the pith, then shred the peel thinly and put in a small saucepan. Add the chopped onion and cold water to just cover. Bring to the boil, simmer for 5 minutes, then strain. Squeeze the juice from the oranges and lemons. Put the juice, red currant jelly and port in a large saucepan and heat slowly until the jelly has melted, then bring to the boil. Add the peel and onion mixture, and simmer all together for about 15 minutes. Make a thin paste with the cornflour and a little water and mix well into the sauce until it thickens. Bring to the boil stirring and simmer for 3 minutes. Cool slightly before pouring into warmed jars. Cover and label. Yields about 1–1½ pts (600ml–900ml). Cumberland Sauce is best served with cold ham, pork or game.

Cranberry Sauce

1 lb (500 gm) cranberries
8 oz (250 gm) sugar
¼ pt (150 ml) white wine or malt vinegar
1 tsp mixed spice
½ tsp salt

Wash the cranberries and cook gently with the vinegar in a saucepan, until the berries are just soft and the skins have burst. Add the sugar, spice and salt and continue cooking, stirring over a low heat until the mixture has thickened. Pour into hot jars and cover. Yields about 1 pt (600 ml).

Mushroom Ketchup

3 lbs (1.5 kg) flat mushrooms
1 dessertspoon chopped onion
½ pt (300 ml) spiced vinegar
3 oz (75 gm) salt

Finely chop the mushrooms, sprinkle with the salt and leave for at least 24 hours. Put the mushrooms and their juices in a large saucepan with the chopped onion and vinegar. Simmer gently for 2½ hours. Pour into hot sterilized jars. The mixture may be strained if wished before potting. Yields about 3 lbs (1.5 kg).

Blackberry Ketchup

3 lbs (1.5 kg) blackberries
Spiced cider or white vinegar
Soft brown sugar

Simmer the washed blackberries, without any water, over a low heat until soft. Rub through a sieve. Measure the puree, and for every pint (600 ml) allow ½ pint (300 ml) of spiced vinegar and 2 oz sugar, (50 gm). Simmer together until thick, stirring often. Pour into hot bottles, sterilize and seal.

Gooseberry Ketchup

1½ lbs (750 gm) gooseberries
1 lb (500 gm) soft brown sugar
¼ pt (150 ml) vinegar
1 tsp cinnamon
1 tsp ground cloves
1 tsp ground allspice

Wash the prepared gooseberries and put with the rest of the ingredients in a pan. Bring slowly to simmer stirring, then cook over a gentle heat for 1½–2 hours. Stir often. Pour into bottles and seal. This ketchup is very good with cold meats.

Vinegars

Most of us are familiar with ordinary malt vinegar, and probably spiced pickling vinegar as well, but many other types of vinegar can be inexpensively made. And it's well worth the effort of doing so because they can really help you ring the changes and create some excitingly different dishes.

Herb and vegetable vinegars are ideal in salad dressings, and sauces, or to flavour fish.

Fruit vinegars can be used as soothing remedies for sore throats, or diluted to make thirst quenching drinks.

Method

Most vinegars are made by infusing a vinegar with the chosen herb or vegetable over several weeks, then straining and boiling. For some recipes the vinegar has to be boiled before adding the flavouring.

Fruit vinegars are made with soft fruits. These are bruised and left to steep in vinegar for 4 days to extract the juice before straining, adding sugar, cooking and bottling.

Equipment

Apart from bottles, screw tops or corks, little equipment is needed except scales, a large bowl, wooden spoons and muslin.

For fruit vinegars sterilize the bottles before closing and seal corked bottles with paraffin wax.

Storing

Stored in a cool, dark cupboard vinegars generally keep very well.

Mixed Herb Vinegar

Mix equal amounts of prepared and chopped parsley, marjoram, tarragon and chives. For every 4 heaped tablespoons of herbs, add 1 pt (600 ml) vinegar. Leave in a covered jar to steep for 3–4 weeks. Strain, bottle and cork.

Onion Vinegar

Finely chop 4 oz (125 gm) of prepared onions, and steep in 2 pts (1.2 litres) wine vinegar for 2 weeks, shaking often. Strain and bottle. Use for salad dressings.

Garlic Vinegar

Peel and crush 8–10 cloves of garlic. Bring 1 pt (600 ml) vinegar to the boil and pour onto the garlic. Steep for 2 weeks, strain and bottle.

Chilli Vinegar

Split 2 oz (50 gm) red chillies in half. Boil 2 pts (1.2 litres) of vinegar, add the chillies and bring back to the boil. Pour into a warmed jar and leave to stand for 5–6 weeks. Strain and bottle.

Mint Vinegar

Wash and dry 1 pt (600 ml) of fresh mint

leaves. Pack into a jar and pour on 1 pt (600 ml) of vinegar. Leave for 3 weeks, strain and bottle. This is useful for mint sauce or salad dressings.

Fruit Vinegars

Currants, raspberries or blackberries make the best fruit vinegars.

Put 1 lb (500 gm) of prepared and washed fruit in a bowl, and crush lightly with a wooden spoon. Pour over 1 pt (600 ml) of malt or white wine vinegar. Cover and leave to stand for 4 days, stirring occasionally. Strain through double muslin. Measure into a pan, and to each pint add 1 lb sugar (750 gm to 1 litre). Stir over gentle heat until dissolved then boil rapidly for 10 minutes. Cool and bottle. Fruit vinegars make a refreshing drink diluted with water or soda water.

Cucumber Vinegar

Peel and finely chop 5 small cucumbers and 2 onions. Put into a jar with 1 pt (600 ml) of malt or white wine vinegar. Cover and leave for 8–10 days, shaking occasionally. Drain off and bottle. Use for cold fish dishes or salad dressings.

Spiced Vinegar

There are three basic methods for making spiced vinegar. If the first method is used, the vinegar must at some point in the pickling or chutney process be boiled, or the preserves will not keep long. The boiled vinegar must be allowed to get cold before adding the pickles unless otherwise stated in the recipe.

1st Method

Using only whole spices, put ½ oz (12.5 gm) each of cloves, cinnamon, white pepper and allspice into a large well corked bottle with 2 pts (1.2 litres) of vinegar. Shake the bottle at least once a week (or as often as you think of it) and steep for 1–2 months. Strain off the spices and bottle the vinegar until required.

2nd Method

Put 2 pts (1.2 litres) vinegar in a saucepan and add 1 oz (25 gm) mixed pickling spices. Cover, and bring slowly to boiling point. Remove from the heat and leave to steep for 2–3 hours, then strain.

3rd Method

Put 2 pts (1.2 litres) vinegar in a saucepan and add 1 oz (25 gm) mixed pickling spices. Bring slowly to the boil and boil for 15 minutes, then strain. Alternatively, the spices can be tied in a muslin bag.

If you like a sweet pickle, add 8 oz–1 lb (250 gm–500 gm) sugar to 2 pts (1.2 litres) of vinegar. For a piquant pickle, add 1 tsp mustard powder instead of sugar.

Tarragon Vinegar

Lightly bruise 1 pt (600 ml) of fresh young tarragon leaves, and put them in a 2 pt (1.2 litres) jar. Fill the jar with vinegar, preferably white wine vinegar, cover, and leave to stand for 3–4 weeks. Strain, bottle and cork tightly.

This vinegar is excellent for salad dressings and white sauces. This method may also be used for other herb vinegars, such as dill, thyme or marjoram.

Drying

Drying

The preservation of food by drying is an extremely ancient craft. Probably not quite as old as that of salting, but still able to boast a pedigree that extends back over several thousand years.

It seems likely that the process was discovered by accident. Man observed that fruit which fell from the trees naturally shrivelled and dried in the sun, and that wild and domesticated animals alike sought out these preserved delicacies with relish when food was in short supply. Naturally enough our common ancestor investigated the phenomena, and like the animals found them tolerably good to eat. In no time at all it would have dawned on him that if he could assist this chance process in some way he could always have a supply of food at hand to draw on through the hungry months of winter.

From these chance beginnings the process would have gradually developed over the centuries; finally becoming what is still today an important method of food preservation. Perhaps more important than most of us would at first realize. Dried fish, fruit and meat are all still produced commercially, and we rely on them to a much greater extent than we might think. For example, life would not exactly be made easier if there were no more currants or raisins would it?

But serious commercial drying is now mainly a pursuit in countries where sunshine can be more or less guaranteed. In less favourable climates it is better to put your faith in artificial heat sources that can be readily controlled.

Method

The principal of drying food is quite straightforward. The object of the exercise is to remove a large proportion of the moisture from the food so that it will stabilize and not deteriorate. This is done by the gentle application of heat. It has to be a gentle application because only in this way can moisture be slowly tempted from the produce without actually cooking it.

The other main requirement of successful drying is ventilation. If moisture is to be efficiently removed it must obviously be able to make as swift a departure from the scene as possible.

All this can be achieved in an ordinary

domestic oven—the heat source—with the door open for part of the time—providing ventilation. The best temperature for drying is 50–60 C/120–140 F or Gas mark ¼.

Equipment

Apart from the oven, you will need muslin covered trays of some sort to lay the prepared produce on whilst it is being processed. You can make special frames with muslin tacked over them if you wish, but suitable trays can be quite easily improvised from wire baking trays.

Some types of produce take up less space in the oven if they are threaded on bamboo rods or wooden dowels and hung inside in that way.

Mushrooms are dried by threading them on strings, so you will need a large needle of some sort, and of course some string.

Apart from airtight storage containers you will need no other special equipment.

Drying Fruit

Apples, pears, and plums are probably the most popularly chosen fruits for home drying; but quinces, damsons, grapes, peaches, and apricots are a representative selection of others that can be tackled with equal confidence.

Preparation

The exact method of preparation varies for different fruits, but those chosen should be in prime condition and just ripe. All must be carefully washed and dried before starting.

Method

Apples: Peel, core and slice into rings about an eighth of an inch thick. Place straight away in a mild brine solution—one dessertspoon of salt to half a gallon of water. This will stop them discolouring and help them to remain crisp. When ready to proceed, remove the rings from the brine and dry them individually with a cloth. Arrange separately either on a muslin tray or on wooden rods, and place in the cold oven. Slowly heat to the required temperature, and then open the oven door slightly. Maintaining the temperature, dry the rings for some five or six hours.

When dry, but still pliable like soft leather,

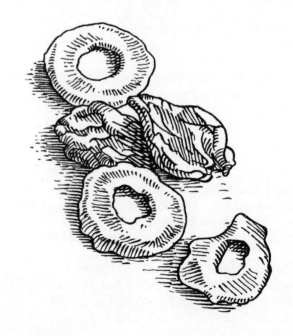

remove the apples and allow them to cool over night in a dark place.

Store in grease-proof paper lined containers in a dry place.

Pears: Peel and core, and cut either into rings or quarters. Then proceed as for apples.

Plums: Depending on their size, either leave whole, or halve and remove the stones; but do not peel or brine them. Proceed with drying in the normal way, but be prepared to extend the time as juicy fruits may require more oven time.

Quinces: Dry in the same way as apples, but do not brine them.

Damsons: Treat in the same way as plums.

Grapes: If you are lucky enough to have your own vines, you can provide yourself with home-grown sultanas. Wash and dry the grapes, and arrange them individually on muslin trays. Then proceed with drying as for plums.

Peaches: Halve and stone, then dry as for plums.

Apricots: Halve and stone, and then dry in the same way as plums.

Storage

Allow all dried fruit to cool thoroughly overnight in a dark place. Then store in grease-proof paper lined tins in a dry place.

Using Dried Fruits

Soak all dried fruits in plenty of clean water for 24 hours before using. Subsequent cooking should be unhurried, with no sugar being added until their preparation is almost complete. Use for pies and puddings.

Drying Vegetables

In the same way that fruits can be bottled more satisfactorily than vegetables, so it is with drying. In fact about the only thing that can be said in favour of doing it is that at least the oven drying times are rather less than for fruits.

Equipment

No special equipment is needed except muslin trays of some sort and a chip basket for blanching the vegetables.

Method

The vegetables are prepared as for cooking, and then blanched in boiling water. String beans then need to be cooled by plunging them into cold water, but this is not necessary for other vegetables. They are then sliced (except in the case of peas), arranged on muslin trays and then dried in the oven for up to 4 hours at 50–60°C/120–140°F or Gas mark ¼.

Preparation & Drying

Onions: Blanch the prepared and sliced

onions for ½ a minute in boiling water. Dry, and arrange on muslin trays or wooden rods. Then dry in the oven for up to four hours.

Carrots: Blanch the whole carrots in boiling water for 5 minutes. Slice, and dry in the oven for around 3 hours.

String Beans: Blanch the beans in boiling water for 5 minutes. Then plunge into cold water, and dry in the oven for up to 3 hours.

Storage

As with fruit, allow the vegetables to cool over night. Then store in greaseproof paper lined tins in a dry place.

Using Dried Vegetables

Soak in cold water for 24 hours before using in casseroles and stews. Cook the vegetables particularly slowly, adding a pinch of bicarbonate of soda to the water to bring out their colour.

Mushrooms

Field or cultivated mushrooms both dry well if they are freshly picked and clean. If they are dirty, wipe them with a damp cloth—don't wash them—and trim off any imperfections.

Method

Mushroom stalks do not dry particularly well, so remove these and utilize them straight away.

Using a large needle of some sort, thread the mushroom tops loosely onto lengths of string, separating each one with a small disc of paper. Particularly large mushrooms can be broken into segments.

Some people now just hang these near a heat source or in direct sunlight, where they will take several days to dry; but the process is probably best done in the oven where it can be better controlled.

Tie the strings across inside the cold oven so that they are freely suspended. The shelf support bars usually make this quite easy to do.

Heat the oven very slowly to around 120 F, open the door, and continue the process until the mushrooms are dry, but still pliable like soft leather. This will take maybe half a day.

Store in air-tight containers in a cool, dark, and very dry place.

Alternative Method

Mushrooms can also be preserved by heating them in a saucepan over a very low heat source until they lose their initial moisture. When they are as dry as you think they are going to get in this way, finish them off in the oven until they are bone dry and crisp. Then they can be pounded to a fine powder and stored in air-tight jars.

Using Dried Mushrooms

Dried mushrooms are normally used only to flavour casseroles, sauces, and soups etc., but those that have been whole dried can be soaked in either milk or water for an hour or two, and grilled and fried in the normal way.

Drying Herbs

Herbs that are not freshly available all the year round can easily be preserved by drying. Pick the young leaves at their summer best after the early morning dew has dried. Strip off any large or coarse ribs and stalks, and tie the leaves into bunches.

Method

Take the bunched leaves and immerse them in boiling water for a second or two. This sterilizes them and locks in their flavour and colour.

If you want, you can now accelerate the drying process by placing the prepared leaves either near a moderate heat source or actually in the oven. But because of their natural fragility and delicate fragrance, this is rather like taking the proverbial sledgehammer to the nut. We find that by far the best and most natural way is to simply set them aside in a warm dry spot and let them get on with it rather more naturally. They do need a little help of course, so place them in securely tied paper bags which will keep dust and mould at bay.

The drying process will take from between seven to fourteen days.

Storing Dried Herbs

Strip the leaves from their ribs and stalks and crumble them in your hands—which should of course be spotlessly clean.

Store them in airtight containers that are impervious to light or they will not only lose their colour, but much of their flavour as well. Which is no doubt why many commercial concerns market them in clear glass jars—so you have to keep on buying a fresh supply.

In a cool, dry place, away from any sort of light source, they will keep in excellent condition for several years at least.

Using Dried Herbs

Herbs are mainly used by adding them directly to the dish while it is cooking, but remove them from their storage container well away from the cooking area or steam may encourage mould growths in the rest of your supply.

In their dehydrated state, dried herbs have a much stronger flavour measure for measure than fresh ones. So if your recipe quotes quantities for fresh herbs, use only half that amount of dried.

Bouquet Garni

These are little muslin bags of herbs that are cooked with soups, and casseroles and anything else that you want to flavour. Traditionally they consist of dried parsley, marjoram, thyme, and a bay leaf. This is probably the most acceptable blend, but there is no harm in varying it a little if not all are readily to hand.

Storage

Make up your own blend, tie in bags, and store in opaque air-tight jars in a cool place.

Salting

Salting

Salting is undoubtedly the oldest form of food preservation known to Western Man. In fact for centuries his very survival through winter would have depended on a staple diet of salted meat, fish, and vegetables. These days, with the widespread use of refrigeration, and all the year round supplies of produce, salting plays nowhere near such a vital part in our lives. But it still has many advantages as a preserving technique. It is cheap and easy to do, and no special equipment or cooking is required. Another advantage is that it leaves precious space in the freezer—if you have one—during the peak harvesting times of late summer and autumn.

Salt

Coarse cooking salt which is bought in block form is best and cheapest. But if you have difficulty in obtaining it, coarse grained sea-salt is equally as good, although more expensive. Some modern food technologists suggest that the iodine content of sea-salt can cause clouding problems, but we have never had any trouble in that direction. On the other hand don't use table salt as the additives in it will make everything go slimy.

Equipment

The best containers are made of glazed earthenware, glass or enamel. Make sure that they are free from chips, and that the necks are wide enough to get your hand into for packing or removing the contents. We use large glass sweet jars, and these are ideal. The lids of our jars are made of bakelite (you can tell how old they are), and it's important that yours are made of something like the same. If metal comes in contact with the salt the contents will be ruined. And don't use metal spoons for handling either, or these may also cause problems. If you have no lid for the container, or one made of metal, a double layer of greaseproof or waxed paper tied around with string can be used.

Salted Vegetables

The most successful salted vegetables are French or runner beans. They taste almost the same as fresh ones. We never seem to have enough peas or cucumbers left over for salting, but both can be treated in much the same way.

One big advantage in salting vegetables is

that they need not all be processed in one go. As long as there is a ½ inch layer of salt in the bottom of the jar, and a layer of salt to finish with, more vegetables may be added every few days as they become ready for picking. As the salt turns to brine, the contents of the jar will shrink and leave space for more vegetables to be added.

Choose only fresh young vegetables, and always use 1 lb (500 gm) salt to 3 lbs (1.5 kg) vegetables.

Store the jars in a cool, dark place to preserve the colour. The vegetables will keep in this way for at least six months.

To serve salted beans or peas, take as many as needed out of the brine, rinse in cold running water, and soak for 2 hours immersed in cold water. Cook as you would the fresh vegetable, but do not add salt.

To prepare nuts for salting, remove the shells and the skins. Discard any nuts that are shrivelled or damaged. To remove the skins, put the shelled nuts under a grill for a few minutes, or blanch them in hot water for 1 minute. Either method will allow the skins to be rubbed off easily with a cloth.

Salted Beans

3 lbs (1.5 kg) French or Runner beans
1 lb (500 gm) coarse salt, cooking or sea-salt

Choose only fresh, young beans. Wash, top and tail French beans, and if they are long, they can be broken in half. String runner beans and slice finely or cut into 1″ lengths. Put ½″ layer of salt into the cleaned, dry jar, then put in a 1″ layer of prepared beans.

Continue with alternate layers of salt and beans, finishing with a layer of salt. Press each layer down well. Cover, and top up the jar every few days as more beans are available, until there is no more room. Store in a cool, dark place.

To use salted beans, take out of the jar as many beans as required, rinse in cold running water and soak for 2 hours in more cold water. Drain and cook as fresh beans, but do not add salt.

Salted Peas

3 lbs (1.5 kg) fresh, young peas
1 lb (500 gm) coarse salt, cooking or sea-salt

Put alternate layers of salt and podded peas into a jar in the same way as for salted beans, starting and finishing with a ½″ layer of salt. Cover and store. To cook salted peas, soak in cold water for 2 hours as for beans, and add a little sugar to the water when cooking.

Salted Cucumbers

4 large or 6 small ridge cucumbers
1 lb (500 gm) coarse salt

Wash and dry the cucumbers and cut into thin slices, including the peel. Put the slices into a broad based, shallow bowl or dish, and sprinkle with ½ lb (250 gm) of the salt. Cover and leave overnight. Next day, drain off the liquid, and dry the cucumber slices in kitchen paper or a clean cloth. Put a ¼″ layer of the remaining salt in a jar, cover with a layer of cucumber. Continue with alternate layers, finishing with salt. Seal and store in a cool place. To use, take out as many slices as wanted, rinse in cold running water and soak for 1 hour in more cold water. Drain well and serve in salads or on their own in a dressing, but do not add salt.

Nuts in salt

Shell and skin the nuts. Put ½" layer of cooking salt into a glass or earthenware container. Pack in the nuts, in layers with more salt, and finish with another ½" layer of salt. Seal with waxed or greaseproof paper and store in a cool place.

Salted Hazelnuts

1 lb (500 gm) hazelnuts
6 tblsp olive or salad oil
2 tblsp sea salt

Shell the nuts and remove the skins. Heat the oil in a heavy-based frying pan, add the nuts and fry gently until they are golden brown. Stir while cooking so that the nuts are evenly coated. Put in the salt and continue cooking and stirring over a low heat, until all the nuts are thoroughly covered with the salt. Turn onto kitchen paper to dry, and when they are cold put in airtight containers.

Caster sugar may be used instead of salt if preferred.

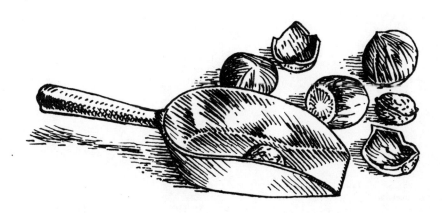

INDEX

Making Your Own Paté

Joyce Van Doorn

Pâté is a savoury mixture of meat, poultry, pulses or fish, sometimes covered with a pastry crust. This book mostly consists of mouth-watering recipes from around the world including dishes not normally described as pâtés in Great Britain such as terrines, mousses, gallantines, rillets, pies and flans.

Author

Joyce van Doorn is a lecturer, writer and broadcaster.

8″ x 8″, 120 pages
Full colour photographic cover
25 line drawings
ISBN 0 907061 01 X   Hardback £5.95
ISBN 0 907061 02 8   Paperback £2.95

Making Your Own Preserves

Jane & Rob Avery

A comprehensive book of over 150 recipes with careful instructions and all the essential background.

Contents

1	Methods, Advantages and Scope
2	General Principles
3	Equipment and Materials
4	Bottling
5	Conserves and Syrups
6	Jams and Jellies
7	Curds, Cheeses and Butters
8	Marmalades, Mincemeats and Crystalized Fruits
9	Pickles and Chutneys
10	Sauces, Vegetable Juices and Vinegars
11	Salting and Drying
12	Meat, Fish and Shellfish

Authors

Rob and Jane Avery are freelance writers specialising in fishing, self-sufficiency and cookery topics.

8″ x 8″, 120 pages
Full colour photographic cover
Numerous line drawings
ISBN 0 907061 17 6   Hardback £6.95
ISBN 0 907061 18 4   Paperback £2.95

The Bread Book

Debbie Boater

A very basic book with fundamental information about the important role that bread plays in our diet and how to make it in its original, nutritious, wholesome form. A wide variety of recipes are included which cover breads, savoury breads, sweet breads, flat breads, pancakes, muffins and pastries.

Author

Debbie Boater is a teacher and founder of the Wholefood School of Nutrition.

8″ x 8″, 96 pages
Full photographic cover
25 line drawings
ISBN 0 904727 95 5   Hardback £5.95
ISBN 0 904727 96 3   Paperback £2.95

Bean Cuisine

Janet Horsley

Bean Cuisine is a comprehensive guide to the cooking of beans and pulses, useful both as a reference book and as a recipe book.

An introductory chapter traces the historic, economic and nutritional aspects of bean cooking, and explains how to use them to make well balanced, nutritious meals. An illustrated A-Z is included to aid recognition, as well as all the information needed to prepare, cook, freeze and sprout the beans.

Author

Janet Horsley is a cookery and nutrition lecturer.

8" x 8" 96 pages
Illustrated with line drawings
Full colour photographic cover
ISBN 0 907061 32 X   Hardback £6.95
ISBN 0 907061 33 8   Paperback £2.95

Making Your Own Liqueurs

Joyce van Doorn

With the help of some simple equipment: a set of scales, glassware, a filter and a mixture of herbs, spices, flowers, fruits, sugar and alcohol, you can make your own liqueurs which will be as exotic and tasty as the commercial varieties. Over 200 different recipes are listed ranging from fruits in alcohol, ratafias, herb and flower liqueurs, to bitters and elixirs.

Author

Joyce van Doorn is a lecturer, writer and broadcaster.

8" x 8", 120 pages
Full colour photographic cover
65 line drawings
ISBN 0 907061 03 6   Hardback £5.95
ISBN 0 907061 04 4   Paperback £2.95

Tea

Eelco Hesse

Tea drinking originated in China and Japan more than 2000 years ago. This book recounts the fascinating history of tea drinking and the colourful development of the Tea Trade over the centuries.

The author also examines the tools of tea making and how tea is grown and processed throughout the world. There is a section on tea blending and full instructions on making a 'perfect cup of tea'. The appendices contain anecdotes, songs and poetry about tea as well as useful addresses for further information and obtaining supplies.

Author

Eelco Hesse is a well-known authority on tea and the tea trade.

8″ x 8″, 120 pages
Full colour photographic cover
Numerous line drawings and engravings
ISBN 0 907061 05 2   Hardback   £6.95
ISBN 0 907061 06 0   Paperback   £2.95

"Making Your Own" Books from Prism Press

Winemaking Month by Month

Brian Leverett

"If you enjoy making wines as well as drinking them you wil find this book both informative and enjoyable. It gives recipes for each month, according to what is in season as well as general guidance on home brewing".
Birmingham Post
"Useful, readable and logically presented."
Do-It-Yourself Magazine

Author

Brian Leverett is a lecturer, journalist and broadcaster.

8" x 8", 120 pages
Full colour photographic cover
37 line drawings and tables
ISBN 0 904727 93 9   Hardback £5.95
ISBN 0 904727 94 7   Paperback £2.95

Home Beermaking

Brian Leverett

This book is more than just a collection of recipes with instructions. It explains clearly, with straightforward diagrams, the complex brewing process and how to achieve the best possible results at home, whether from a can or with the traditional ingredients. The unique fault finder chart will help you overcome many of the problems that you may have had with previous attempts at home brewing.

Author

Brian Leverett is a lecturer, journalist and broadcaster.

8″ X 8″, 120 pages
Full colour photographic cover
32 line drawings and tables
ISBN 0 907061 07 9 Hardback £5.95
ISBN 0 907061 08 7   Paperback £2.95